Privileged Witness

Stories of a local pastor

John Henson

Cover Design   Mike Henson
ISBN   978-0-9561996-0-7
Contact E-mail   johnhenson14@aol.co.uk

Dedicated to
Clare, Michael and Gemma,
Timothy and Judith,
David and Emma

Contents

Introduction

Adventure
My Story

"We have a new student with us this morning by the name of John Henson," announced my biology teacher, Mr Cranswick. He then looked directly at me and said, "I hear that you are a good rugby player!"

That comment to me immediately gave me credit with the other students, and it endeared me to this teacher who was also the first team rugby coach. I would be working harder for him than for any of the other teachers! I had two terms work to catch up as my former school had not had a biology syllabus. Mr Cranswick instructed his best student to lend me all his work, so that I could copy it all in order to catch up. That student's name was David Taylor and he became my best friend.

Leaning over me one practical lesson when I was dissecting a platana frog, Mr Cranswick made a comment that set my heart on becoming a surgeon. He said, "You have very steady hands! You will make a great surgeon!"

Six months later I was sitting between two of my other friends listening to a Church of England evangelist preaching in the Dutch Reformed Church hall in the town of Fort Victoria, Rhodesia. It was April 1st, 1970. The preacher was giving a powerful Gospel message. He was vividly describing the crucifixion of Christ when God spoke to me. Having been brought up with the Book of Common Prayer I had repeatedly addressed Jesus Christ as *"the Lamb of God that takes away the sin of the world"*. Now God was telling me that the Lamb of God had taken away my sin. It became intensely personal. He took my place and bore the full penalty of my sin. He died my death that I might live His life (eternal life). As He had surrendered His life for me, He now was asking me to surrender my life to Him. I was to give back to Him what He had given me in the first place – my whole life!

There and then I closed my eyes, and, overwhelmed by His matchless love for me, I humbly asked Him to forgive my past and come in to my life as my personal Saviour and Lord. I surrendered my whole life to Him, and instantly a peace that I cannot describe filled my being. Tears began to run down my cheeks as I said for the first time ever, "I really love You, Lord Jesus!"

Some time later the preacher closed his sermon with these words, "God is calling sinners to trust Jesus Christ His Son to be their Saviour and to surrender their lives to Him as Lord. We are going to sing the song '*I surrender, I surrender all; All to Jesus I surrender, I surrender all,*' and as we do so I want all who intend to give Jesus Christ their all to make your way out to the front here where my helpers will lead you individually in prayer."

I immediately thought that my surrender had already happened, and that I did not need to go to the front. However, just as the organist began to play the preacher said, "I need to warn you that Jesus said that '*whoever denies Me before men, him will I deny before My Father in heaven; and whoever confesses Me before men, him will I confess before My Father in heaven.*' By coming to the front you will be confessing Him before men."

As the singing began, I turned to my friend James on my left and asked him if he would join me. He said he was already a Christian. I turned to his brother on the right and asked him to join me, and he said, "Sure I'll join you", as if encouraged by my invitation. As we made our way to the front, we noticed many more making their way there too. The preacher encouraged us all to pray 'the sinner's prayer', and we were soon being individually counselled and prayed for by the preacher's helpers.

When I left that building I was "floating on air"! My whole world had changed. Everything seemed different. I felt both a deep sense of satisfaction and excitement at the same time. I had fallen madly in love with Jesus Christ!

What followed surprised me. I was overwhelmed with a desire to tell the whole world about my Saviour. Yes, He was the *"Lamb of God that had taken away my sin"*, but He was also *"the Lamb of God who takes away the sin of the whole world"*. My first thoughts turned towards my parents and siblings. At all costs they too must experience God's love as embodied in Jesus Christ.

I also thought of my friend David Taylor. I knew by now that he was suffering from a degenerative bone disease, and that he had been given six to twelve months to live. About a month after that meeting where I had surrendered my life to Christ, the local Pentecostal Church invited the school and others to a Billy Graham film in the school hall. This was my opportunity to introduce David to his Saviour. He accepted my invitation, and we watched the film together.

I could hardly sleep that night as I thought about leading David to Christ. The next morning I walked to his home praying all the way that he would become a Christian too. He invited me into his sitting room and we sat together on the sofa.

"You know that I am a Christian?" I asked.

"Yes, I do," he replied, "And I want to become one too!"

My dreams were coming to pass. I confessed that I was a brand new Christian myself, and that all I could do to help him become one was to retell some of the message I'd heard from the evangelist and recite the sinner's prayer I had prayed. David was more than happy to do that, and whilst I was reciting the sinner's prayer with him repeating it after me, he began crying, and so did I. There was an awesome atmosphere as I witnessed the amazing transaction between sinner and Saviour.

I then told David about the joy and privilege of prayer, of my ferocious appetite for the Bible, and of my new Christian friends and church. When I left his home about an hour later, I stopped on the road, looked up to heaven and said, "Lord Jesus, You know that my heart was set on becoming a surgeon. Please Lord, would You rather call me and equip me to be an evangelist? What I have witnessed You doing with David this morning I want to witness throughout the rest of my life."

Shortly after his conversion, David's parents pulled him out of school, and they moved to the Eastern Highlands of Rhodesia where, some six months later, Jesus called my first convert home. Twenty-two years later I moved my family to Horsham in the UK, and in the first week of his schooling in England my eldest son, Michael, struck up a deep and lasting friendship with a fellow-Christian in his class. His name is David Taylor!

My pastor soon recognised the call of God on my life and gave me the awesome responsibility of leading the church youth group. That translated into much prayer and much Bible study and rapid growth as a Christian. However I struggled to witness to non-Christian friends and especially my family. My one friend delighted in finding minor moral lapses in me and then calling me a hypocrite.

I was beginning to despair when I met Gordon and Mercia at an inter-church outreach meeting in Shabani, Rhodesia. They were full and running over with the love of God and His boundless joy. I soon made an appointment to visit them at their home.

"You definitely have what I am longing for," I told them. "I have never met anyone with such a joyful relationship with the Lord, and I want you to tell me how I can get what you both have. I feel at times such a hypocrite, and I am a woeful witness to the Gospel of Christ."

"We were there once," began Mercia. "That was until we received from the Lord Jesus the baptism of the Holy Spirit."

"So were the first disciples of the Lord," said Gordon. "They were behind closed doors for fear of the Jews – and that was despite the fact that they had spent the previous three and a half years with Jesus. Then, on the day of Pentecost, they were all filled with the Holy Spirit, and they received the fearlessness that launched Christ's church. The Baptism of the Holy Spirit enabled them to live the Christ-like lives that won their world for Christ!"

"This is all quite new to me," I admitted. "Could you give me a Bible study on it?"

"Certainly," said Gordon, "If you have an hour to spare right now, we can take you through the relevant Scriptures. Mercia will write down the verses so that you can take them home and prayerfully go over them again yourself."

When the Bible study was over, Mercia prayed a most meaningful prayer over me and, just as I was about to leave, her daughter Faith appeared from her bedroom. She was in my class at school. Whilst I knew she was a Christian as she attended the school Scripture Union with me, I did not know she was a pastor's daughter. Mercia explained to her that I was enquiring about the Baptism of the Holy Spirit, and she joyfully exclaimed, "I have the perfect book for you to read!"

She rushed back into her bedroom, returning moments later with *The Cross and the Switchblade* by David Wilkerson. By the end of the week I finished that wonderful book. It convinced me that what I was missing was indeed the Baptism of the Holy Spirit. I also reached the last chapter of the Gospel according to Mark. When I read *"these signs shall follow those who believe…in My name they shall speak with other tongues"*, I looked on the notes Mercia had written out to find Gordon had not mentioned this Scripture. I could not wait to show it to him!

So the next morning I phoned for another appointment to see him. I left home at about ten in the morning. I was a long-distance runner, so I began to run the two miles to Gordon's home. The route took me past the school. As I reached the entrance of the school, I noticed that our little dog was following hard on my heels. I stopped and told her to go home. She refused. I shouted at her, and she cowered but refused to return home. Exasperated, I said to God, "Lord, if You want me to go to Gordon and Mercia to receive prayer for the Baptism of the Holy Spirit, please take my dog home!"

When I opened my eyes I just could not believe what I saw. Coming out of the school gates was my dear mother. "I have no idea why I am going back home," she said, "But I am sure to remember when I get there!"

"Could you take Trixie home?" I asked. "I am just off on a run to see the Jacksons."

"Certainly, son, but don't be late for lunch!"

God answered my prayer! When I arrived at Gordon and Mercia's home I was very excited and expectant. I opened my pocket Gideon's Bible at Mark 16 and showed Gordon the verse I had read the night before. "Have you ever seen this verse?" I asked excitedly.

What Gordon said was so gracious that I have never forgotten it. "Isn't it so wonderful that God showed you that verse Himself!" I later discovered that he knew almost half the New Testament by heart!

"Please could you pray for me to receive the Baptism of the Holy Spirit?" I asked.

"I would love to," said Gordon, "But the Bible gives us an order for things, and I would like to show you that." Then opening his Bible to Acts 2 he read, "'Repent, and let every one of you be baptized in the name of Jesus Christ for the remission of sins; and you shall receive the gift of the Holy Spirit'. You have repented, John, and what remains for you is to be baptized in water, and then you will receive the Holy Spirit."

I protested that I had been baptized as an infant. He explained that that was really my parents' dedication of me to the Lord, and that baptism in the New Testament was for repentant believers. I asked for a study, and he and Mercia sat down with me for another hour. Although I was convinced, I needed time to process the news, especially since my own church practiced infant baptism.

By the following Saturday I was so convinced about the need to be baptised by full immersion that I put on my swimming costume under my trousers, and I ran back to the Jacksons' home, fully expecting Gordon to take me in his car to the nearest river and baptize me there. To my great disappointment he told me that I was underage, and that he would need to ask my parents' permission. I was ready to give up as I was sure that they would be upset, not understand and say no. Gordon told me to trust the Lord, adding that God sees my heart and was sure to make a way. "What is more," he concluded, "It will give me an opportunity to witness to your parents."

The appointment was made, and Gordon met with my parents. When he left they kept commenting on what a wonderful man he was. His respect for them and his whole manner had convinced them to entrust me into his hands for baptism in water. "We do not know why we are consenting," my dad told me, "I guess we don't want you to miss out and then resent us."

Now that my parents knew, I would have to let my pastor know. So I arranged to see him and decided I would ask him to baptize me. When I told him he burst into tears. It was the first time I had seen him cry, and I apologized for upsetting him. He complained that I had not studied what he believed on baptism, and I promised him I would delay until he could explain it to me. He gave me J.C.Ryle's book on Anglican Theology, and in the following week I read the relevant chapters. By the end I was more convinced than ever that Gordon was right, so I went to see my pastor with the request to God that, when He wanted me to go ahead with baptism, my pastor would say, "Go ahead John!"

He did. I phoned Gordon, received assurance from him that I would not have to leave my church and join his, and set the next Sunday as my big day.

My whole family came to my baptism. I was very nervous giving my testimony in front of them and a new congregation. The water was freezing, it being mid-winter. I came out feeling so fresh and clean! After

I had changed into dry clothing, I sat in a chair in the front row to receive prayer for the cherished Baptism in the Holy Spirit. I felt very nervous as my family were sitting in the row behind me. Gordon noticed that and calmed me with gentle assurance and then out of my mouth came the most beautiful prayer-language. I was now speaking as the precious Holy Spirit was giving me utterance. When I stood up and faced the congregation I was told that my face radiated real joy! I was transformed and my witness for Christ went to a whole new exciting level. So many people commented on my joy and asked why. One lecturer at university called me "the grand-piano" and when I asked why he said, "Because you are always showing your keyboard!"

Mercia had given me the Scripture about *"those who honour Me, them will my Father honour"* before my baptism and God proved true to His word. That evening my mother re-dedicated her life to Christ and within the next two weeks both my brothers and my one sister had surrendered themselves to Christ's Lordship. My mother wrote to my older sister at university telling of our testimonies and she wrote back saying that she could not wait to come home for the July vacation. She wanted what we had found and within a week of her vacation she too became a born-again Christian.

I was asked by my pastor to leave my church. He did not want me to influence his youth group or any others in the church so I joined Gordon's church and loved it. The following January I began my science degree at the University of Natal in South Africa. I joined a Pentecostal church and the first Bible studies I attended were on how to lead someone to repentance toward God and faith in the Lord Jesus Christ. From there we went out every Wednesday night door-knocking. I could tell of so many stories of those adventures.

The terror war had begun in Rhodesia, and as my dad was a District Commissioner, his life would daily be at risk. So every prayer-meeting I would intercede for his salvation. Then the night before we left for home for the July vacation the Lord spoke to me through the gift of prophecy. He said, "My servant John Henson, these holidays you shall see the one near and dear to you coming in." I wrote it down and dated it.

When we returned home my dad decided that he would come along to church with us. At the door I showed Gordon my prophecy. It really excited him, and he encouraged me to reverently claim God's promise in prayer. That service my dad came under such conviction that on the way home in the car, he promised us that the next weekend we would be at the cottage at Lake Kyle, and not in church.

His arrangements fell through, and he was back in church the next Sunday, and the next, and the next. I remember going into the church that Sunday saying to God that this was His last chance to fulfil His word to me. Gordon preached on the Holy Spirit, and at the end of the service made an appeal for surrender to Christ and for the baptism of the Holy Spirit. My dad responded.

When Gordon reached my dad, my dad asked for prayer for the Baptism in the Holy Spirit. Gordon explained to him that he first needed to humble himself in repentance and trust Jesus Christ to be his Saviour. There and then my proud dad yielded himself to Him who sacrificed His life for his salvation, and he was born-again. At the door, as we were leaving the church, my dad asked Gordon if he could baptize him before my sister Ann and me returned to university that coming Thursday.

Gordon arranged for the baptism to be held at the Bible study on the Wednesday night but phoned when we were having our traditional Sunday roast to arrange for it to happen that night. So that night my dad was baptized in water and in the Holy Spirit and God proved faithful to His promise.

I could tell of so many stories of my university years, of the students who came to faith whilst we were there, of the healings and gifts of the Holy Spirit. One story I must tell is of the vision of hell that God gave me. It fired me up to such an extent that to this day I feel enraged whenever Christian leaders down-play evangelism.

I was on my knees praying when God gave me a very clear mental picture, or shall I say movie. I was standing on a small grassy hill looking down a narrow path that I knew I had travelled and was on. At the beginning of the narrow path there stood a narrow gate. I knew I had come through that gate. On either side of that gate there was a fence and beyond that fence was a broad way running parallel with the fence. In the broad way was an innumerable mass of people all moving in the same direction. God then took me amongst that crowd, and I recognised real people there. I recognised a few relatives, a few university students and lecturers, and a few school friends. Suddenly God lifted me out of the crowd, and instinctively I knew He was taking me to where they were all headed. I screamed out to God, pleading with Him not to take me there. But He did, and tears fill my eyes every time I recall what I saw there. There was a precipice. People were tumbling over it. Some seemed to be caught by surprise; others saw it and tried to fight their way back up the broad way. God took me beyond the precipice, and I could see flames of fire. They were like giant arms with hands that grabbed those falling off the edge and pulled them down with force and speed. I felt they were claiming their victims as if they had a right to. I was by now beside myself with anguish. I felt that my heart could burst, and I screamed out to God to stop the flow of humanity.

I will never forget what happened next. At the base of the arms of flame was black darkness. It was so black that if someone placed their finger two millimetres from their eye they would not see it. It was also deathly silent. I remembered how once Mercia told me that the Bible says the wicked shall be silent in darkness (1 Samuel 2:9). She contrasted that with that glorious Psalm which says, *"You have turned my mourning into dancing; You have put off my sackcloth and clothed me with gladness, to the end that my glory may sing praise to you and not be silent. O Lord my God, I will give thanks to you forever"* (Psalm 30:11,12). Some people I have told this vision to have pointed out that Jesus warned that there would *"be wailing and gnashing of teeth"*. I tell them that even those are silent!

Shortly after that vision I was leaving the dining hall, when I was accosted by a fellow student who had a number of his friends with him. The friends encircled me, and he said jokingly, "John, please don't try to persuade me to go to heaven! You see all my friends here? They are all going to hell, and I want to end up where my friends are."

As I looked around at all those sniggering students my eyes filled with tears, and so turning to him, I said, "The Bible describes hell as outer darkness, so you will not even see your friends!"

His mouth opened in preparation to say something but no words came out. The sniggering stopped abruptly, and one by one the students sulked off. I wonder to this day whether the Holy Spirit used that encounter to put each of those students on the journey to turn to Jesus Christ to save them.

I told the vision to Pastor Colin, who immediately told me that he must get me preaching the Gospel. He told me to come with him each Sunday afternoon for a month to the four Zulu churches around Pietermaritzburg. At the first two he would preach so as to show me how it is done, and the next two he would have me preach so that he could assess whether I was up for it. After the final Sunday Pastor Colin, the one who taught me how to win the lost to Christ, released me to preach every Sunday afternoon.

I would go to Edendale, a high density African township, to collect Enoch my interpreter. From there I would either preach at the Edendale Church, the Howich Church, the farm Church near Richmond, or the Valley of a Thousand Hills Church. I was also doing door-knocking in Peitermaritzburg, and at one of the homes I witnessed a man, who happened to be high up in the South African Police Force, come to Christ. A year later he found out that I visited Edendale every Sunday afternoon. He told me that that township was crawling with communists who were armed and extremely dangerous. The police would only go there in convoy and fully armed! What was worse was I was taking Clare along with me! We thanked God for His protection, and for the remainder of our time at university we continued as we had done before.

At the Zulu churches we witnessed many coming out of their spiritual darkness into Christ's marvellous light and life. We also witnessed some remarkable healings and deliverances. I remember one amazing healing. A middle-aged lady stood before me and through Enoch told me of excruciating pains in her shoulders. Just as I was about to lay hands on her to pray for her healing, I remembered that Jesus rebuked the fever in Peter's mother-in-law. I felt I needed in like manner to rebuke the pain in this lady's shoulders. It went against all my scientific understanding of pain, but, I thought, there were no critical people there so it was worth the try.

"I rebuke this pain in these shoulders in the mighty Name of Jesus Christ!" I said with authority. The lady screamed and held her stomach. Enoch told me that the pain had moved to her stomach. Now I knew I was on to something, so I again rebuked the pain, and this time I commanded it to leave her altogether. She screamed again and held her hips.

The pain went to the knees, then the feet and finally left her. It was then I noticed that she had strings of beads around her neck, her wrists, and her ankles. I asked her why, and Enoch told me that the witchdoctor had given her the beads to keep the evil spirits in her so that they would not torment her children. I then asked her to remove all her beads as the spirits had now left her, and I told her that she needed to trust the Lord Jesus for her protection and the protection of her family.

What happened next took me by complete surprise. As she stood up straight after removing the last beads from her ankles she buckled over, as if hit in the stomach by a fist, and screamed in agony. Now the whole congregation erupted, as I angrily commanded the spirits to leave her alone for good. She gave a big sigh, straightened up and smiled from ear to ear.

Twenty nine years later I was back in Pietermaritzburg to preach, with Clare, at a Zulu church conference. I was met there by the District Minister who immediately recognized me. "I know you," he said, "I was seventeen years old when you were preaching at our church in the Valley of a Thousand Hills. I will never forget the deliverance and healing of Mrs Ncube. The pain and torment never came back to her!"

What was so interesting too about that conference was that I stood up to preach on winning our lost world for Christ to a packed school hall on October 1st 2005 – exactly twenty five years to the day when I began full-time ministry for Jesus Christ at my first pastorate in Redcliff, Zimbabwe. As a way of celebrating that anniversary the Holy Spirit brought another twelve precious blood-bought souls to the Saviour!

Chapter 1

The Power of a Return Visit
Tom and Kay's Story

Peggy, a pastor's wife with a real pastor's heart, phoned me one morning. "John," she began, "I wonder whether you could be so kind as to visit someone for me?" Peggy lived in Gweru, a city some 150 miles south of Harare. "Her name is Patricia, although she prefers to be called Trish. She is a quadriplegic, and she is being cared for at the Knaphill Nursing Home in Hatfield, Harare. I gather she does have a faith of sorts."

"Certainly Peggy," I replied, "I would love to do that for you. Please pray for me as I visit her."

I phoned the home to establish the best time to visit. As a clergyman I could visit outside of visiting hours. I was given the following morning at 11am. When I arrived I checked in at reception and was directed out into the garden and told that Trish was in her wheelchair under the Msasa tree. They offered me a plastic chair to take with me to sit on. I was warned that Trish was blind and had a voice impediment, but could hear perfectly.

"Best that you sit down first before you introduce yourself and begin speaking," the receptionist added, "And you will need to listen very carefully if you want to understand what she has to say."

I felt overwhelming compassion for Trish as I sat down on the plastic chair right up close to her wheelchair. She was very hunched up with her head bowed down.

"My name is Pastor John Henson, Trish, and I was asked by Peggy in Gweru to come and visit you."

All I received in reply was a grunt. Although I pleaded in my heart that God would give the words to say, I found talking to Trish was like wading waist deep through treacle.

"This is very kind of the nurses to wheel you out into the garden to sit under this magnificent tree where you can feel the gentle summer breezes" and "I guess you enjoy listening to the different bird songs out here too," were two of my somewhat corny lines.

The grunts coming from Trish deeply unsettled me. They indicated to me that she was not prepared to put any effort into communicating with me. I sensed that Trish was very bitter, desperately lonely, and I feared she felt totally abandoned by God. I knew nothing of her background and felt God telling me not to ask about her family nor tell her of mine. I hated the awkward silences between what I found myself saying. "This is going nowhere!" I thought to myself, so I resolved to ask her whether I could pray for her, and then I would take my leave.

"I need to go now Trish," I said. "But before I go, may I ask you whether I could pray for you?"

"OK, if you like," she replied.

I discerned that she agreed more out of politeness than faith. I proceeded to ask God, "Lord, please wrap Your arms of love around Trish so that she is fully aware of Your loving and compassionate presence with her through her trials and difficulties. Thank You for the cross of Calvary which is infallible proof of Your everlasting love for us all."

I laid my right hand on Trish's bony shoulder as I rose from the chair. "God bless you, Trish," I said as I picked up the chair to return it to reception.

"How did you get along with Trish?" asked Lynn, the owner and nurse-in-charge of the home, who happened to be at reception when I returned.

"Difficult!" I admitted, "I would however really like to know more about her. Are you able to fill me in? What brought on her awful condition?"

"Trish is now 39-years-old," Lynn replied, "I know she looks a lot older. Two years ago she went in to have her fallopian tubes cut and tied in a sterilization operation. The gynaecologist performing the operation cut the tube from her only functioning kidney to her bladder instead of the fallopian tube. She went into a coma, and another surgeon re-operated to fight for her life. Her condition now is the result."

"That is just so tragic!" I exclaimed. "Does she have a husband and children?"

"Don't you dare talk about her husband!" Lynn warned. "He has a mistress, and although he occasionally brings their two children to visit her, he never speaks to her himself. No! Don't you dare speak to her about her husband."

"What about parents?" I asked.

"Oh she has lovely parents," said Lynn.

"Do you think they would mind if I contacted them? Maybe visited them too?" I asked. I had this growing feeling that God had not finished with Trish yet. He wanted a return visit, and this time I'd be much better informed and prayed up. Lynn willingly gave me Tom and Kay's phone number and said, "I know you will like them. I imagine Trish was really lovely too, before this tragedy!"

I phoned Tom and Kay that evening and was warmly invited to visit them the following evening. They were indeed lovely people. They adored Trish but harboured deep bitterness towards both the gynaecologist and Trish's husband.

"Trish was having marriage problems," Tom told me. "She had been hearing rumours that her husband was having an affair. She had confronted him, but he denied it. In fact the rumours turned out to be true."

"That's the mistress who lives with him now," chipped in Kay. "He has the audacity to make the children call her 'mom', and we are now 'rationed' with our time with them!"

"What about Trish's faith? Peggy in Gweru asked me to visit Trish saying that she believed she had a faith," I interjected, hoping to divert them from spilling out their bitterness. At this point I was assuming that Tom and Kay had faith in God and understood what I was asking.

"We advised her to go to church where we hoped she would find the help she needed to put her family back together," was Kay's reply. "She went down to that church in Stony Road on the Sunday before that tragic operation. Poor darling, our hearts are broken for our daughter. She is so very lovely. Why did this have to happen to her? It is so unfair! If it was to happen to anyone it should have happened to her husband and his mistress."

"You've seen her, Pastor Henson," said Tom. "She is a broken person. Not just physically but also emotionally and spiritually. She is so bitter and twisted and moody. We visit her often, and although we know she is grateful for our visits, we sense she wants to die and spare us the trouble."

"Knaphill Nursing Home has been wonderful," said Kay. "I truly admire them for their patience with Trish – especially when she gets in one of her moods. Her moods can last weeks. It is hard work to visit her then as all we get from her are grunts."

She must have been in one of those moods for my visit, I thought.

The next day I revisited Knaphill Nursing Home. Trish was in her wheelchair under the same Msasa tree in the garden. I pulled up the plastic chair to sit next to her and said, "Trish, this is Pastor John Henson, I have come back to see you."

Trish began to cry, and soon she was sobbing. It caught me completely off guard. I had never anticipated such a reaction.

"I am so sorry if I have upset you, Trish. Please forgive me!" I looked around quickly to see if anyone had noticed what had happened, and if there was anyone who could help me! We were alone. No one from the home came. Then, to my great relief, she composed herself.

"You have not upset me," she said. "No, I am crying because you are the first church minister to ever come back to see me."

"I came back because I have been to visit your wonderful parents. They told me all about what has happened to you, and I have felt compelled to return to assure you that despite the tragedy and injustice of it all, you are greatly loved by God. In fact, right now I feel overwhelmed by the love God has for you." I sensed that a truly amazing thing was happening right there and then. I remembered how in the Book of Acts the Bible says *"God opened Lydia's heart."* God Himself was opening Trish's heart!

"Please tell me about God's love," said Trish with not a trace of cynicism. I must admit that prior to my visit I had wondered how I was going to be able to convince her of God's unfailing and everlasting love, given all the terrible things that had happened to her. I recall the inner voice instructing me to tell her all about Calvary's cross. Now, having God open her heart, she was genuinely asking me to describe His love for her.

"The greatest proof and indeed the greatest demonstration of God's love are found at the cross of Calvary," I began. "You see, Trish, God in the Bible gave us laws to keep, laws such as *'to love the Lord our God with all our hearts and to love our neighbours as we love ourselves'*. We have all failed to consistently keep those laws. Now, no law is any law unless there are penalties for breaking that law. The penalty for breaking God's law is death. By that the Bible means eternal exclusion from the presence of God. In other words – it is hell. The only way God could satisfy Himself that that penalty should not be borne by you and me is if He paid the penalty. So He substituted Himself for you and me on the cross of Calvary. He bore your sin and mine and was punished in our place. Before He died on that cross, He cried with a loud voice *'It is finished!'* which was a colloquial term meaning 'It is fully paid!' He wants us to believe that. You can tell Him that you believe by inviting Him to be your personal Saviour. By doing that Trish, you will be forgiven your sin, God will make you His own child, and He will give you His life, which is eternal life. You will then enjoy a relationship with Him whereby you will know He is really with you through all your trials and hardships."

God had indeed opened her heart, and Trish was very eager to pray with me the sinner's prayer inviting the Lord Jesus Christ into her life, yielding her life to His benevolent Lordship. I cannot describe the exhilaration I felt as I witnessed "the great transaction". The Lord Jesus came into Trish's life, and He transformed it.

I visited Trish almost every week for about six months after her conversion. Then, owing to other commitments, that changed to once every two weeks. I will never forget how she used to laugh and laugh with excitement when she heard my footsteps on the gravel pathway leading from the car park to the home. I would share with her the Scriptures, and often what I had preached the previous Sunday. I always ended my visit with a prayer for her, her parents, her children and the nursing home. (And yes, she did want to know all about my wonderful wife and sons). Many times I prayed for her healing.

Some eighteen months after her wonderful conversion, Lynn called me from the home. Trish had gone into total renal failure and was in a coma. I did not get to her in time to say goodbye. She was a truly beautiful person, despite outward appearances. Her chief beauty came from the intimate relationship she enjoyed with Her Saviour and Lord. Lynn cried over the phone. "The light has gone out, the light has gone out at this home!" she said. "It was after your second visit to her that she was transformed. From then Trish filled this home with her infectious joy and we will never be the same without her!"

I knew Lynn meant every word she said. I knew what she said was true!

I conducted Trish's funeral. Warren Park Crematorium Chapel was packed out. Twenty or more people stood just outside the doors. I was thrilled to witness her popularity. Tom and Kay sat in the front row. Trish's husband and her two beautiful children sat some three rows behind them. A woman I presumed was his mistress sat with them.

We sang *What a Friend we have in Jesus, all our sins and grief to bear.*

I delivered the eulogy in which I included Trish's wonderful conversion story, repeating what I had said to her that led to her acceptance of Jesus Christ as her Saviour and Lord. I quoted what Lynn had said about the light and joy Trish brought to the home after her conversion. I explained that for a Christian like Trish, death was like the blowing out of a candle at the dawn of a bright new day. I read out Bible verses such as *"We are confident, yes, well pleased, for to be absent from the body is to be present with the Lord"* and *"In Your presence is fullness of joy; at Your right hand are pleasures forevermore"* and *"Eye has not seen, nor ear heard, nor has entered into the heart of man the things which God has prepared for those who love Him"*.

I know that I was bold to say this, but I said, "I dare to say to you all, based on what the Bible has to say, that unless you have a similar conversion experience to Trish, you will never see Trish again."

We sang *The Lord is my Shepherd*, I thanked God for every remembrance we had of Trish, and prayed God's comforting presence for all who keenly felt her loss. I then committed her broken body to the elements after I had pressed the button that lowered the coffin out of sight.

I led Tom and Kay out of the chapel and stood with them on the concourse where I shook the mourners' hands as they proceeded out of the chapel. Some were silent; others thanked me for "a lovely service". Lynn called me aside to announce to me that she was closing the Knaphill Nursing Home.

"Lynn, you must not do that!" I protested, "You run a wonderful home....What about the other patients?"

"As I said to you, John, the light at Knaphill has gone out! I cannot see myself continuing without Trish." She and I were in tears. I gave her a little hug, and she silently walked away to be joined by some of her nursing staff who embraced each other before all climbing in their car. Although I did phone Lynn the next week, I did not ever see her or Knaphill again.

Tom and Kay had invited everyone back to their home for light refreshments after the funeral service. About twenty people milled around in their lounge and dining room. The mood was sombre, and I was pensive. Although Tom and Kay expressed gratitude to me, I felt they were very subdued, and I did wonder "how well had I done for them?" I phoned them a few days later, and they assured me that they were coping all right and, no, they did not feel they needed a visit.

A year later, Kay phoned me. "Pastor Henson," she said, "this is Kay, Trish's mother."

"Hello," I replied, "How are you?"

"Not very good, I am afraid. For a month now Tom has been asking me to call you for a visit. We went down to Tshipise in South Africa for a week to mark the anniversary of Trish's death. On the way there and on the way back Tom pestered me to phone you. We have been back at home now for a week, and yesterday Tom began to swell up all over. He is now at the Pariwenatwa Hospital, and I am desperately worried about him. Please could you visit him this afternoon?"

"Certainly, Kay! Could you let me know what ward he is in, and I'll be there at 3.30 this afternoon."

She told me the ward and said she looked forward to seeing me there. I took with me my favourite book for people who are seeking after God – *The Cross and the Switchblade* by David Wilkerson – and the tract called *The Four Spiritual Laws* by Campus Crusade for Christ. Kay was there by Tom's bedside, and so were three or four others. Kay vacated her chair for me, and I spoke to Tom first about his physical condition and then about his spiritual condition. I was afraid for him, as I felt sure that God had given him a premonition that he did not have long to live. I also remembered how I had warned the congregation at Trish's funeral to become Christians or else never hope to see Trish again. I felt that that warning had become a signpost that God had placed in Tom's heart to point him to Jesus Christ.

"Tom," I said after asking about his condition and what the doctors were diagnosing, "If you were to die tonight, do you know for sure that you will go to be with Trish in heaven?"

"No, I must admit, I am not at all sure," was his honest reply.

"Tom, the Bible says that it was written that we may know that we have eternal life. However, before I share with you from the Bible how we can know for sure we'll go to heaven when we die, may I ask you another question?"

"Sure, go ahead," he said.

"If you did die tonight, you stand before God, and He asks you 'Why should I allow you into My heaven?' what do you think would be your reply?" I asked.

"I really do not know! I think I would throw myself onto His mercy!"

"The only thing that will keep us from heaven is our sin." I continued, "The Bible defines sin as the breaking of God's law. The Bible declares that all have sinned, and the penalty for our sin is death. We can never clean ourselves up for God. The good news is that God so loved us that He gave His one and only Son to be our Saviour. He became our Saviour by going to the cross of Calvary where the Bible says 'He bore our sins in His own body on the cross.' He took the punishment we all deserve for our sins. He wants us to believe that and to invite Jesus Christ into our lives to forgive us our sins and give us His eternal life."

Just then a nurse arrived to take Tom's blood pressure and temperature. This distraction was enough to throw me. I felt the moment of decision was lost. I believed that I would need Tom on my own, and I vowed to myself that I would visit him again outside of visiting hours. After the nurse left I gave Tom *The Four Spiritual Laws* and *The Cross and the Switchblade* saying that I believed they would help him enormously to understand the Christian message.

Tom allowed me to pray for him. I prayed for his healing, and I prayed for the Lord to make Himself known to him, giving him the faith to trust Him for his salvation.

That was Saturday. The next day I was busy in the morning with our morning service, and we had visitors for lunch, and they stayed with us long into the afternoon. Just before the evening service Kay phoned me. "Pastor Henson, I am desperately worried about Tom. He has been transferred to the Cardiac Care Unit. He has been diagnosed as having heart disease. I don't know what to do!" She began sobbing on the phone.

"I have an evening service that is just about to begin," I replied. "How about if I come around to your home immediately afterwards, and we pray together?"

"I would really appreciate that, Pastor Henson. What time can I expect you?"

"Eight o'clock if that is alright with you?" I answered.

I pulled into her drive at eight, and she came out to greet me. Back in her home she poured me out a cup of tea, and we discussed her husband's condition. She apologized for calling me out and explained that her one son lived in the USA and the other in South Africa. She had not been a "church-goer", I was the only minister she knew, and I had helped Trish so much when she was alive. She was terrified that she might be now losing her husband whom she adored. The atmosphere in her living room was charged with her emotional pain.

I offered again to pray for Tom and her. She agreed, and we both bowed our heads. As we did so I sensed God's awesome presence. "I know that You are here, Lord," I began. "And I know that You love and care about us far more that we could ever appreciate or understand. Kay and I humbly place into Your hands her husband, Tom. Please make him fully aware of Your presence there in the Cardiac Care Unit where he is. Please grant him a gift of healing! Please restore him to his dear wife. Please give to both Kay and Tom Your perfect peace. We ask these things in the precious name of Jesus Christ our Lord. Amen."

"Thank you so much," said Kay, wiping away some tears from her eyes and cheeks with a tissue. She too had sensed God's wonderful comforting presence.

The next morning the Henson household was all up early as usual. Michael aged four and Tim aged two were our organic alarm clocks. It was usually my privilege to take Michael to his nursery school but that morning a strange reluctance to do so came over me, so I asked Clare to take him instead. Tim went along for the ride.

Just as Clare drove out of the gate, the phone rang.

"Am I speaking to the Reverend John Henson?" asked the caller.

"Yes you are."

"I am calling from the Cardiac Care Unit at the Pariwenatwa Hospital. I have with me Kay. Her husband is in a critical condition so I have asked her who her minister is, and she has given me your name and phone number. Please could you come immediately?"

"I'll be leaving right away and will be with you as soon as I can!" I said as I was looking for the church car keys. I ran out to the car, raced to the hospital some two miles away, jumped out of the car and ran into the hospital and down the long corridors to the Cardiac Care Unit. I was quite out of breath when I was greeted by the nurse and shown to Tom's bedside.

Although Tom was in a coma I knew that the last faculty to go was his hearing, so I took him by his hand and said, "Tom, this is Pastor John Henson. I have come to pray with you so that you will find peace with God through our Lord Jesus Christ."

I began to pray for him. "Lord Jesus!" I said from my heart, "Please do not allow Your sacrificial death on the cross for Tom to have been for nothing. Please save him by Your amazing grace. Grant him the faith to believe in You and to believe that You offer him forgiveness for all his sin. I praise You for your mercy! Amen."

I then addressed Tom. "Tom, I know that you can hear me. Please pray this prayer after me. 'Lord Jesus, I am so grateful that You came to save me from my sin. I believe that You took my sin and were punished in my place when You were crucified. I am so sorry for my sin and humbly ask You to forgive me. I surrender my life to You as I trust You now to be my Saviour. Please make me Your child and give me Your life – eternal life. I now praise You, Lord Jesus, Amen."'

Just as soon as I said "Amen," Tom began to gasp for breath. The one nurse exclaimed, "I think we are losing him" and she, with a swoop of her right arm, ushered us out of the room whilst the other nurse began working on his chest. I stood with my one arm around Kay's shoulders and her one arm around my waist in the adjacent room.

"Thank you," she whispered and then fell silent.

The door swung open and the nurse stood there with tears in her eyes as she said, "He waited for you to say that prayer! After my phone call to you and whilst you were on your way here we had to revive him. It did not work this time. God bless you! God bless you both!"

Kay now swung around to hug me and cry into my chest. "Thank you," she whispered again. "I prayed the prayer you prayed with my husband, and I just know that we'll be with each other – and with our beloved Trish – for ever and ever! Thank you so very much! Thank the Lord!"

I gazed up towards the ceiling with tears flowing down my cheeks as I silently worshipped our Saviour for His saving grace that pursues a sinner to death's door! In my heart I sang that line from a famous old hymn *Hallelujah! What a Saviour!*

Kay became a faithful and joyful member of our congregation until one night, years later; she succumbed to heart disease and joined her Tom and her Trish in the eternal presence of her Saviour.

I also remember how that, before Kay died, I was returning home from visiting her when I believe God spoke to me. It was not an audible voice but a "still small voice" or conviction in my heart. I had just passed a road when I felt strongly that I should turn back and visit Jill who lived in that road. My immediate reaction was to question the leading. I did not visit young married women on my own. She held a good job so why would she be at home now? She had not been back to church since a few weeks after she married Graham two years before.

By the time I reached the tee-junction the conviction was so strong that I turned around and made my way to her home. As I parked the car on her gravel driveway I was overcome with fear. This did not look good. What if her husband found out? I had thought that he had been responsible for her pulling out of church, so what would he think? Now I was there, there was every chance that any occupant of the house had seen me come in or heard the car wheels on the long gravel driveway. I felt trapped.

"Here goes," I said to myself as I opened my car door. "Please, Lord, may I have got this right!"

I rang the door-bell and within seconds the door swung open. There stood Graham! My mouth went dry, and I could not speak. My worst fear had come to pass. How do I explain this visit?

"I cannot believe this," he said shaking his head. The tone was not angry but surprised. I attempted to say something but couldn't, still feeling I may have overstepped the line.

"Come on in," he said, moving aside for me to pass him. "I cannot believe this!" he said again.

"As I was passing your road I felt a compulsion to come here, so I turned around at the tee-junction and came."

"Just three minutes ago Jill told me that she wanted to see a pastor! That must have been when you were passing our road! This is incredible! You won't know this, but Jill has been bedridden with anorexia. We have booked flights to London, leaving tonight. She has been very anti-church for nearly two years now. She just expresses a desire to see a Pastor and in minutes you arrive. Incredible!"

Graham ushered me through to their bedroom, and there lay Jill, her face sunken in and her arms wasted away. Seeing me, she burst into tears. Graham repeated what I had said to him.

"Thank you for being obedient to God," she said. "You have no idea how much this means to me!" She began to cry again and then went on to explain that she had deliberately walked away from God. She was full of remorse, and she was amazed that God had not given up on her.

"I would like to pray for you, Jill," I said. "Calvary's cross tells me how much Jesus loves you, how much He wants to hold you and relate to you. You have been a wonderful Christian. You know how to ask Him to forgive your sin and come back into your life. I'll pray for you after you have prayed."

Without hesitation Jill closed her eyes, bowed her head, and talked to her Saviour. I stood there in tears as I witnessed this intimate transaction. I then laid my hands gently on her forehead and prayed earnestly for God's deliverance and healing. I had such a strong sense that God would answer that prayer just as he had answered her desire to see a pastor. We talked for a while before I left. Graham thanked me profusely for coming, and I prayed silently that God would reel him in to His kingdom.

A week later I met Jill's mother in town. "Have you heard from Jill?" I asked.

"Yes, John, and guess what?" she replied.

"What?"

"She ate the dinner and the breakfast on the overnight flight to London, and Graham did not have to take her for the treatment she went over there for! God has healed her of her anorexia!! I am so very thrilled – the nightmare appears to be over for us all!!"

Chapter 2

"Where is He?"
Angie's Story

Clare and I met Angie at the back of the church after a Sunday morning service. She appeared to be very nervous. "It has been wonderful to have you here this morning. Is this your first time here with us?"

"Yes! This is my first time here," she replied, looking first at us and then away, as if she needed to survey the rest of the church.

"Did you have a particular reason for coming here this morning?" asked Clare, hoping to engage her in a conversation.

"Well actually, I did!" she exclaimed as she looked back at us with that look that asked, "Are you both interested in what I want to say and will you be able to really help me anyway?"

"Would you like to tell us about it? We would like to be able to help," I said.

Angie looked around again to see whether others would be listening in and then said, in hushed tones, "I've been quite spooked by what I've seen going on in the house that my first floor flat overlooks. The tenants have these candle-lit meetings with several guests around their dining room table. In the daytime before the meetings I have noticed a number of puppies running around the back garden. After the meeting the tenants go out into their back garden with these little bundles which they then proceed to bury. The next day there is not a puppy to be seen!"

Noticing the pained look on both Clare and my faces, she asked, "Can you tell me what is going on? Is this some kind of satanic ritual where they sacrifice puppies? What kind of sick people would do such things? I assure you that I am not making this all up!"

"We believe you Angie! We are truly sickened by your story. These things do happen, and there are a lot of Satanists about. In ancient times they would sacrifice children – even their own!"

By now other people in the church were beginning to make their way to the back of the church so as to exit the main doors. Some wanted to greet Angie, and others wanted a word with either Clare or I, so I offered to visit Angie in her flat. She was delighted, and we set a date and time.

On arriving at her front door, Angie immediately ushered Clare and I through her lounge and onto her balcony that overlooked the neighbouring house. We could see partially into the dining room where the meetings would take place. The lights were on, but there was no activity.

"I hope I did not give you the impression that they have those meetings every night. They probably happen once a month. One happened last Friday night. On Saturday I found your advert in the local and decided to go to your church for some answers." Angie then hastily ushered us back into the lounge and offered us tea and cake. She was obviously nervous about her neighbours seeing us there.

I had just taken my first sip of tea when Angie said, "John!" I looked up to see her staring me straight in the eye. "My husband had too much to drink at a pub a couple of miles from here. Despite that, he drove himself back home. Well, he lost control of his car and crashed it into a tree, killing himself." She paused, I suppose to see what impact this news had on me, before slowly and very deliberately asking, "So where is he now?"

Her news and subsequent question caught me completely off guard. At the same time, I felt a crushing responsibility to represent Jesus Christ effectively to her. What I replied could open or close the door to her heart. I knew instantly that I had to get it right.

She had asked me and not Clare. I knew that I could not even give

Clare a sideward glance. Angie was looking intently at me. From my heart I called on the Lord for help.

The prayer seemed to only take a second. Almost simultaneously I recalled two verses from the Bible.

"The Bible says that in the last days the sun will be turned into darkness and the moon into blood before the coming of the great and awesome day of the Lord, and it shall come to pass that whoever calls on the name of the Lord shall be saved," I said as I noticed Angie hanging on every word. "When your husband's last day came and the sun for him turned to darkness; if in his dying moments he called on the name of the Lord, then according to the Bible, he would have been saved by God's grace. The Lord would have accepted him into heaven."

I then proceeded to describe heaven, quoting verses such as *"In His presence is fullness of joy, at His right hand there are pleasures forevermore"* and, *"Eye has not seen, nor ear heard, nor has entered into the heart of man the things that God has prepared for those who love Him."* I told her of God's promise to wipe away every tear from their eyes; that there would be no more death, nor sorrow, nor crying. There shall be no more pain, for the former things will pass away. He will make all things new.

Angie was listening intently to me. I could feel it. It then hit me that she knew about hell – the so-called "other place" – and she knew that there was every possibility that her husband had not called on the name of the Lord. False hope would not answer her question, nor bring her real comfort. She did not say a word. She wanted a full reply, and she was looking to me to give it.

I knew that Clare was faithfully praying for God's wisdom to be given to me. I really felt that, and my heart was truly grateful. God answered our prayers, and this is how:

I remembered the story that the Lord Jesus told in Luke 16. I proceeded to tell Angie, "The Lord Jesus told us about a certain rich man and a certain beggar called Lazarus. Lazarus died and was carried by the angels to Abraham's bosom. The Lord Jesus later told the repentant dying thief on the cross next to His *'today you will be with me in paradise'*. It's the same place – the place of the departed believer before the Lord Jesus was resurrected and took paradise to heaven. The rich man also died. He went to the other section of Hades that Jesus describes as the place of torment. When the rich man lifted up his eyes he saw Abraham afar off and Lazarus in his bosom. Then he cried and said, *'Father Abraham, have mercy on me, and send Lazarus that he may dip the tip of his finger in water and cool my tongue; for I am tormented in this flame.'*

"Abraham explained to the rich man that there is a great gulf fixed between the place of torment and where he and Lazarus were. No one can cross that gulf. The rich man then begged Abraham to send Lazarus back to his father's house, saying that he had five brothers whom he wanted Lazarus to warn, *'lest they also come to this place of torment.'*

"Angie, whether your husband is in heaven or the place of torment, I believe he will be praying that someone would come and share the gospel with you and warn you, so that when your time comes, you go to heaven and not hell." At this point I looked across at Clare and then back to Angie before saying, "I believe that Clare and I are the answer to that prayer."

Instantly, I could see on Angie's face that what I had said had sunk in. There was an eagerness about her as she leaned forward and said, "Please show me how to become a Christian."

"That would be our greatest privilege," I replied without being able to hide the joy that welled up from deep inside me. The Holy Spirit had wonderfully opened her heart. I took out my Gideon's New Testament from my pocket and Clare took out her New Living Testament from her bag. Clare sat beside Angie pointing to the Bible verses that I was reading so that Angie could see the Gospel message herself.

Angie admitted that she was a lost sheep that had gone astray. She saw that God had laid on His Son, Jesus Christ, her sin and rebellion. He had paid her penalty in full when nailed to that old rugged cross. She accepted Jesus Christ as her personal Saviour, inviting Him to come into her life to cleanse her from her sin and make her whole. She surrendered the rest of her life to His lordship. She became a "born-again" Christian that night, with a deep assurance of her salvation and a profound comfort in her grief.

Chapter 3

Complete Healing
Jim and Joan's Story

Andrew phoned me on the Wednesday morning, "Pastor John," he said, " I have been sharing my faith with this lady called Joan. Will it be alright to bring her along to Bible study this evening?"

"Of course it would be alright, Andrew," I replied.

I had first met Andrew at university over six years before that phone call. My friend Ian had invited his friend to church, and he had said that he would only come if Andrew came with him. For a laugh Andrew did come with him. Andrew confessed afterwards that he scorned everything done in church that night. However, during the appeal for new converts, I had been moved by God to operate the gift of tongues. Although Andrew did not respond to the appeal, he was struck with awe and wonder, and as soon as the service was over he went to Ian to ask what was being said by me.

"Was that Latin that guy was speaking?" he asked.

"No," said Ian, "That was a supernatural gift from God called the gift of tongues. You can read all about it in 1 Corinthians14."

As soon as Andrew returned to his room at our halls of residence, he took out the Bible his mother had given him and, turning to 1 Corinthians 14, read all about this phenomenon he had witnessed. He then rushed around to Ian's room to ask him how to become a Christian. Ian that night led Andrew into a personal relationship with the Lord Jesus Christ.

Andrew dropped out of university at the end of that year and he returned to Rhodesia where he passed the very rigorous selection course for the Rhodesian SAS. He served with distinction in the SAS for some five years. Immediately after independence in April 1980, the new Zimbabwean government disbanded this very efficient and effective fighting force. Many of Andrew's comrades left the country but Andrew remained behind, living now with his parents and trying to adjust to civilian life. Clare and I met up with him that October when we began our first pastorate in the small town of Redcliff.

Andrew was so hungry for God and His Word. He would take himself off into the hills near Redcliff where he would sleep rough and spend time reading the Bible and praying. He would then come to me with all sorts of theological questions, and we would pour over the Scriptures for answers. Fresh out of Bible College, I found my times with him very refreshing and challenging.

Joan came with Andrew to our Bible Study. We were examining the fruit of the Holy Spirit. When our study ended we went into a time of prayer. That is when Andrew said, "Joan has been suffering from severe back trouble for about three years now. Could we pray for her healing?"

"Certainly," I replied, and looking at her I said, "Do you mind if we put you on a chair in the middle here, and we all gather around you, we lay our hands on you, and we trust God together to heal you?"

"That is very thoughtful of you," she said as she stood up from her chair to walk over to the one now placed in the centre of the room. I prayed for God to touch her from head to foot and heal her of all her back trouble. Andrew also prayed. Everyone else said "Amen" at the end of sentences. I really felt God's presence with us as we prayed.

"How is that?" I asked, hoping that she had been instantly healed.

"I feel very peaceful, thank you all very much," was her reply.

The next morning Andrew phoned me with great excitement. He had just come off the phone with Joan. She told him that when she woke up that morning she felt no pain or discomfort in her back. She managed to climb out of bed without any difficulty and then, miracle of miracles, she was able to bend down and put on her slippers herself for the first time in three years. God had healed her completely, and she and her husband Jim wanted to come to church on Sunday to give thanks!

Joan was so full of gratitude and excitement when she met me at the door of the church that Sunday. She introduced me to her burly husband who also thanked me for the prayers for his wife "which had worked!" He looked quite unsure that he wanted to be in this unfamiliar place with these unfamiliar people. He relaxed a bit when Andrew came up and greeted them and offered to sit with them. Others in the church also greeted them and they soon settled down.

It was a very special service, that Sunday. God made His awesome presence felt as He especially does when new people come seeking Him. I spoke of the greatness of God with special emphasis on the greatness of His love as displayed in His substitutionary death on the cross of Calvary. At the close of my sermon I said, "Jesus Christ gave His life for you, thus paying in full the penalty of your sin. He did that so as to win you for Himself. He wants to forgive you so that He can enjoy an everlasting relationship with you. He gave His life for and to you so that you would give your life to and for Him. Will you do your part and turn your back on your own way, to embrace Him and His way? If so, please, whilst every head is bowed and every eye is closed, raise your right hand so that I can pray for you."

Joan raised her right hand. Jim must have felt her movement. He turned his bowed head towards her, opened his eyes and then lowered his head again. He made no response but it was clear that his journey to Christ had begun that morning too. Clare and I prayed for and with Joan after the service. She left church a committed Christian with a deep desire to live the rest of her life for the Lord Jesus.

In a follow up visit the next week, Joan told us this remarkable story. "About five years ago," she began, "Jim and I visited Harare for the weekend. It was there that we bought a soapstone sculpture of a baboon, and we gave it to our son in Kadoma on our way home. It was after that that his marriage began to fall apart, ending in a very acrimonious divorce, and he lost custody of their son. Then just over three years ago he was killed. You see, he was a member of the Police Anti-Terrorist Unit, and his 'stick' of men was called out to a sighting of terrorists. They left the armoured personnel carrier and went on foot patrol for a few hundred yards when they were pinned down by heavy enemy fire. He could see that they were greatly outnumbered, so he wiggled his way back to the armoured personnel carrier in order to drive into the ambush site and rescue his men. He traveled barely one hundred yards when the front wheel detonated a boosted land-mine, and our son was instantly killed. We had the grim task of settling his affairs, packing up his belongings and selling his home. We brought that baboon sculpture back here. That is when I put my back out and suffered with back trouble until my healing last Wednesday night."

"Where is that sculpture now?" I asked, sensing that it could be carrying the curse of a witchdoctor or spirit medium.

"The gardener has smashed it to pieces," she said. "Jim and I have recently returned from a holiday down south. Whilst we were away we had a burglary. Our neighbours then took it on themselves to ask Andrew to stay in our home until we returned. One night he was awakened by a clattering noise coming from our living room. So he picked up one of Jim's golf clubs and made his way down the passageway to the living room, expecting that he might encounter an intruder. As he entered the living room, he said he saw the baboon sculpture with real eyes staring back at him. He shouted something and switched the lights on and the 'real eyes' disappeared. The next day Jim and I returned. Andrew told us about his experience and warned us to get rid of the sculpture. We were travel weary, I suppose, and, if we were to be honest, we were skeptical. So we did nothing about the sculpture until last Wednesday morning."

"What changed your mind?" I asked, interrupting to show that I was fascinated by her story.

"The same thing happened to me as happened to Andrew. Jim was on night shift at the steelworks and I was at home alone. I heard a commotion in the living room, so I went to Jim's bedside-table, took out his service revolver that he has had since he was a pilot in the Second World War, and made my way down the passageway to the living room. To my utter astonishment, there was the baboon sculpture looking at me with real eyes. I was terrified! I screamed and then, remembering what Andrew had told me, I switched on the lights, and those scary eyes disappeared. I left those lights on all night, and in the morning I called in the gardener to ask him to get rid of the sculpture."

"What did he have to say?" I asked.

"Well, he told me that the sculpture was evil. I asked him what I must do with it, and he said, 'You must smash it in pieces, madam!' So I asked him to do that, and that is what he did. He took it outside, and with a sledgehammer he smashed it to pieces! I then phoned Andrew, and we talked for ages. Later he phoned me to invite me to your Bible Study."

"I believe that there is a definite link between that sculpture and all the terrible things that happened to your son and then yourself with your back trouble. After you had it smashed, God stepped in and healed your back, and then on Sunday He healed your heart by forgiving your sin and taking up residence there. What does Jim think of all this?"

"God certainly has Jim's attention now!" Joan replied. "He can see the link you are talking about; he can see the change in me, and he is asking a lot of questions. He says that he is very impressed at the sincerity and friendliness of the members of your church. He is really happy for me too. You mentioned water baptism on Sunday. Can you tell me more about that? Do I need to get baptized to become a member of your church?"

"We do not make it a stipulation that a person has to be baptized to become a member of our church," I said. "Baptism is a wonderful public confession of your faith in Jesus Christ. What you are symbolizing is firstly your belief that Jesus Christ died, was buried and rose again from the dead. Secondly, you symbolize your belief that Jesus Christ died for you personally, that He was buried for you personally, and that He rose for you personally. Thirdly, you are symbolizing that you have been crucified with Him or, put another way, you have died to your self and your old way of life, you have buried it in a watery grave, and you have risen to live a new way of life – His way of life."

"What do you mean by 'watery grave?'" she asked. I realized that she probably thought that baptism was by the sprinkling of water as in infant christening.

"The word *baptizo* in the Greek actually means 'to immerse'. Let me read Acts 8 verses 34 through to 39 for you," I replied, reaching into my pocket to bring out my Gideon's New Testament and turning to the passage. *"So the eunuch answered Philip and said, 'I ask you, of whom does the prophet say this, of himself or of some other man?' Then Philip opened his mouth, and beginning at this Scripture, preached Jesus to him. Now as they went down the road, they came to some water. And the eunuch said, 'See, here is water. What hinders me from being baptized?' Then Philip said, 'If you believe with all your heart, you may.' And he answered and said, 'I believe that Jesus Christ is the Son of God.' So he commanded the chariot to stand still. And both Philip and the eunuch went down into the water, and he baptized him. Now when they came up out of the water, the Spirit of the Lord caught Philip away."* I paused to see whether she was taking it in.

"If they both went down into the water it could not have been sprinkling because that could have been done from a water container," she reasoned out loud, "So the eunuch was immersed. I see!"

"Immersion is the only way to understand the symbolism contained in baptism," I added. "You probably also noticed that Philip said *'belief with all your heart'* is a pre-condition to baptism. Peter, after his first sermon, told those who had asked him what they must do, to repent and be baptized. You have repented and believed so you, Joan, qualify to be baptized. Besides this, you have promised to follow the Lord Jesus, and He was baptized solely to set an example for His followers. It will be a great witness to Jim too."

"Let me give it some thought, Pastor John," she said, "and let me talk it over with Jim tonight. The last thing I want to do is antagonize him. I already feel I would love to be baptized. I will let you know soon."

Joan phoned me the next morning to tell me Jim was quite happy with her decision to be baptized so could I baptize her as soon as possible. I asked her to read Romans 6:1–11 and excitedly told her we would baptize her in Trevor's swimming pool after our morning service that Sunday. I advised her to bring a large towel and a change of clothes. We would provide a thick white robe for her to wear. I talked to her about giving her testimony. I told her that just before I lowered her under the water I would say, "Joan, on confession of your faith in the Lord Jesus, and at your own request, I now baptize you in the Name of the Father, the Son and the Holy Spirit." Her testimony needed to be a confession of her faith in the Lord Jesus.

It was another special morning service that Sunday. At the end of my sermon I gave an appeal to anyone present who wanted to surrender his or her life to Jesus Christ to pray a prayer after me quietly in his or her heart. I felt that if I asked the seeker to raise their hand that Jim would think I was gunning for him, and he would resist. After praying the "sinner's prayer", pausing after every few words, I asked that if anyone prayed that prayer, he or she should let me know after the service. I closed the service, gave directions to Trevor and Esme's home, and we drove there for the baptism.

Before going down the swimming pool steps, I gave a brief explanation of the symbolism enshrined in this great public witness, and Joan gave a brief but meaningful testimony. She spoke of her meeting and talking with Andrew; of her attendance at our Bible study at Trevor and Esme's home; of the healing to her back; and of her surrender to the Lordship of Jesus Christ the previous Sunday. She knew He had forgiven her all her sin and made her His daughter. She wanted to follow Him everywhere He would lead her, and she knew that He had led her to confess Him in baptism.

I took her by the hand down the steps until we were waist-deep in the water. I prayed for her and then baptized her. As I lifted her up again the church members clapped and clapped. I looked over to Jim who looked very proud of his dear wife. He had joined in the clapping. She looked radiantly happy. As she came out of the water, Clare was there to wrap the large towel around her and congratulate her.

Whilst the congregation was having tea, and after Joan and I had changed, Clare and I prayed with Joan to receive the Baptism of the Holy Spirit. To our great disappointment, Joan did not show any sign of having received Him. However, when we came out to mingle with the congregation again, Jim came over to me to announce that he had said the sinner's prayer during our morning service. We were overjoyed, and we took him into the living room to counsel him to receive assurance of salvation and basic instructions on beginning a life with the Lord Jesus.

Two weeks after her baptism, Joan asked to see Clare and I. She told us that she had a most embarrassing problem. She was a teacher at a secondary school, and both in the classroom and the staff room she would have total lapses in her memory. Her mind would just go blank, and it frightened and embarrassed her. Could we pray with her? Then she added, "Pastor, I believe my problem is spiritual. I don't know why, but I think it is an evil spirit that is troubling me. It could be linked to that baboon sculpture we had."

I admitted that I had not thought of that possibility, but it would explain why there was no sign that she had received the baptism of the Holy Spirit after her baptism in water. "Alright," I said, "We will come against this evil spirit in the Name of Jesus, and we will trust the Lord Jesus to deliver you."

Clare and I stood in front of Joan. We did not lay hands on her as we do when praying for healing. We braced ourselves for the fight. "Lord Jesus," I began, "We pray that You be the centre of what we are about to do, and that You grant to us the authority we need to command any evil spirit troubling Joan to forever leave her. Please protect us during this task. We look to You to bring deliverance and freedom to Joan through us. Thank you, Lord."

I opened my eyes, looked at Joan and then with an authoritative tone in my voice said, "In the Name of Jesus Christ of Nazareth, we command any evil spirits troubling Joan to leave her right now! We plead the Blood of Jesus for Joan and against you! We bind you in Jesus' name and command you to leave!"

Joan winced, shot up her hands to cradle her head, shook her head and gave out a piercing shriek of pain for a few seconds.

Then she calmed down with a sigh.

"What happened to you, Joan?" I asked.

"I felt like some terrible force squeezed my head and then released it. I have never felt such intense pain like that before!" Joan sighed and then smiled broadly and peacefully. "John and Clare, I believe it has gone! That evil spirit has gone! The Lord has set me free! Praise the Lord! I feel so relieved."

"Praise the Lord!" Clare and I said in unison. Then I offered to pray again for her to be filled with the Holy Spirit. "God wants to fill you with His Holy Spirit not only to ensure that this evil spirit that has troubled you can never return, but also so that you have the power to live a victorious Christian life."

"I would so appreciate that Pastor," she said bowing her head in readiness for prayer.

I opened my Gideon's New Testament and turned to Luke 11:13 and read, *"If you then, being evil, know how to give good gifts to your children, how much more will your heavenly Father give the Holy Spirit to those who ask Him!"* I turned to Acts 2:38,39 and read, *"Then Peter said to them, 'Repent, and let every one of you be baptized in the name of Jesus Christ for the remission of sins; and you shall receive the gift of the Holy Spirit. For the promise is to you and to your children, and to all who are afar off, as many as the Lord our God will call.'* God has called you Joan, so the promise of the Holy Spirit is for you! We would like you to ask your heavenly Father to fill you with the Holy Spirit, knowing how much He wants to give Him to you. He will fill you as He promised you. Acts 2:4 reads *'And they were all filled with the Holy Spirit and began to speak with other tongues, as the Spirit gave them utterance.'* You may find that as you are praying in English, other words come to your lips that are not English. That will be a wonderful sign that God has indeed filled you. Apart from having the same experience as all one hundred and twenty disciples we read about in Acts 2:4, you will have a prayer language that you can use every day in the future to pray in God's perfect will. Clare and I will also pray for you, first in English and then in the prayer language the Holy Spirit has given us. Are you ready for that?"

"Yes I am," she replied, and bowing her head, she asked her heavenly Father to baptize her in the Holy Spirit. She went quiet so Clare and I laid our hands on her and prayed, "Heavenly Father, we pray that You will fill Joan with the Holy Spirit. We pray that You will fill her with your love, joy, peace, long suffering, gentleness, goodness, faith, meekness, and self control. Grant her too the gift of her own prayer language as a definite sign that she has indeed been filled with the Holy Spirit. In Jesus' name we pray, Amen."

Clare and I then began to pray in our prayer languages, and to our great joy, Joan soon followed. We all raised our hands in worship. It was a most wonderful experience, and Joan was overjoyed. She could not stop smiling and giggling. That night Jim phoned to say, "Whatever God has given Joan, I would like!"

In response to that I did a Bible study with him both on water baptism and the baptism of the Holy Spirit. I baptized him that Sunday, and he was baptized in the Holy Spirit after his baptism, when his expectancy was at a peak.

Jim and Joan were a great blessing to our congregation for a further year, after which he retired from the steelworks and they left for their smallholding in the Eastern Highlands of Zimbabwe. Andrew was with us for three months before he left to study at the same Bible College in South Africa where I had studied.

Chapter 4

The Power of Forgiveness
Helen's Story

Some time after Joan's deliverance from that evil spirit, I was in discussion with three pastors at our weekly pastor's prayer meeting. The topic raised was "can a Christian have a demon?" I recounted Joan's experience telling them that it was a carry over from before her conversion, and that it really happened, and she was now really free. She had had no more lapses in her memory; no more blackouts. Stuart, one of the pastors, then told of a very difficult member of his congregation. He had wondered whether she had ever had a genuine conversion experience.

"Our discussions this morning and Joan's testimony make me think that she, too, has evil spirits troubling her. If I set up an appointment to see her, would you mind coming with me?" he asked.

"Sure!" I said.

The following week Stuart and I were sitting in Helen's garden having a cup of tea with her. After the initial polite conversation I looked at her and asked, "Is there any way Stuart and I can help you?"

"Well! I am a child-basher!" she said as she looked first at me and then at Stuart. She paused long enough to take in our reactions and then, because we both kept quiet, she continued, "I never wanted to be one!"

"Are you telling us that you were bashed as a child yourself?" I asked.

"How did you know? How did you know?" she replied, looking at Stuart accusingly, as though he must have told me beforehand.

"It was actually the way you said 'I never wanted to be one.'" I replied, regaining her attention, "I imagine that as a young child you vowed that when you had your own children, you would never treat them like you were being treated."

Helen then recounted how her father would often come home drunk, and he would beat up not only her and her sister, but also their mom. She had made the vow not to do that to her own children; yet, when they had exasperated her she found herself repeating her father's out-of-control behaviour. She would shout and scream first, but that soon turned to violence.

"I hate myself for what I do to my children. They cower in the corner of the room like I used to with my father," she said, looking at the grass in front of her and then away at the clouds in the sky. "When I lose control, I really lose it!" Then glaring at me she spat out, "You are a pastor. You are meant to have all the answers! Tell me – what can I do?"

I admit that I was taken aback at the harshness of her tone. Was this an evil spirit talking through her? It struck me as uncouth and abrasive. I asked the Lord again for wisdom and discernment, and then calmly said, "You can begin by forgiving your father."

"What a joke!" she sneered back and shaking her head in disbelief asked, "How can I do that? He died years ago!"

"At the moment you are making him accountable to you, Helen. Your unforgiveness has imprisoned you. Release your father into God's hands, and he will become accountable only to God, and you will be set free!"

What happened next was truly amazing. She believed me and asked for prayer to help her forgive her father. Sensing that the garden was not appropriately private, we made our way into her living room for the time of prayer. By the time she sat down in the armchair she was in floods of tears. God was doing an amazing work in her. His Fatherly presence seemed to fill the room. I prayed that God would enable her to release every childhood abuse by her father into His hands; every failure to intervene on the part of her mother, into His hands, together with all her father's drunkenness and ill treatment of her mother and sister. As I prayed, Helen's sobbing grew louder, and she kept repeating, "I forgive him!"

I suddenly felt anger at the evil spirits that had ridden on Helen's father's back and now were riding hers. I asked for God's authority and protection over Stuart, the household and myself. Then looking over Helen's bent over body I said with an authoritative tone, "You foul abusive spirits, I bind you in the almighty Name of Jesus Christ of Nazareth and I command you to leave Helen right now. The blood of Jesus Christ which is for Helen is against you, so leave – right now!"

Helen coughed and gave a deep sigh and her shoulders shook just a little. She then looked up at me and said, "I think they have gone. Thank you so much! I feel quite different. Everything feels different!"

"Praise the Lord," both Stuart and I said after each other.

"We need to pray that God fills you with His Holy Spirit now, Helen, so that those horrible spirits are never able to return again. He will help you change completely; He will give you the love and the wisdom to properly discipline your children. Pastor Stuart here will also be a great help to you if you will ask his advice."

We prayed again for her and left. The next week we did a follow-up. We were met at the gate by one of Helen's friends who asked, "Are you the pastors who prayed for Helen last week?"

"Yes, why do you ask?"

"You know there has been such a dramatic change in her that the domestic worker asked, 'What has happened to the madam? She is so quiet! Is she sick?'"

Helen then came out to meet us with these memorable words, "It's a miracle! I am so different now! Do you know that I now find it hard to even raise my voice to my children, let alone pick them up and throw them against the wall?"

"God has been just so very good to you Helen! We pray that He'll give you all the wisdom you need to raise your children to love and appreciate Him too!" I replied.

Helen remained a loyal member of Stuart's church and I had no further dealings with her. As far as I know, her transformation was permanent, and for that I give our Saviour and Deliverer praise!

Chapter 5

Enough Time
Bill and Mavis's Story

Cybil came to our church one Sunday with her cousin, May. Seeing a new face in the congregation, I was careful to include in my message how to become a Christian, and at the end I gave an appeal. She did not respond, and I did not labour the point. She returned the following week, and although she did not respond to the Gospel message then, she willingly accepted my request to visit her in her own home.

There, over a cup of tea I asked her, "Do you know for sure that were you to die tonight you would go to heaven?"

"No", she replied, "I did not know anyone could be sure,...I certainly hope so!"

I told her that I could show her from the Bible how we could be absolutely sure but first I needed to know, "Should you die tonight and then stand before God, what would you answer Him if He were to ask you why He should allow you into heaven?"

She went on to explain to me that she would probably tell Him that she had lived an upright life, been a good neighbour, and given to charities. She was aware that she was not perfect – "but then nobody is!"

I explained to her that we have all broken what the Lord Jesus said was the great commandment, namely, *"to love the Lord Your God with all your heart, with all your soul and with all your mind."* We all therefore stand in need of God's forgiveness. To make this forgiveness possible, God chose to bear the punishment due to us for our sins. This He effectively accomplished on the cruel cross of Calvary. The Bible says that Jesus Christ bore our sins in His own body on the cross. He died our death so that we could live His life. What He requires of us is to believe in His way of salvation by accepting that we cannot by our good works save ourselves.

I was sitting in one chair and I moved to another one saying, "If that chair represents my good deeds and this chair I have moved to represents Jesus Christ, then my moving to this chair represents the transference of my faith from my good deeds to the Lord Jesus. We need to accept Jesus Christ as our personal Saviour, asking Him to forgive us our sins – those things we have thought, said, or done that fall short of perfection – and surrender our lives to Him."

I asked her whether she understood. She did.

I then asked whether she would like to place her trust in Jesus Christ and surrender her life to Him.

"Yes!" she said.

Delighted, I showed her from my pocket Gideons' Bible 1 John 1:9 and John 1:12 and I invited her to pray with me, repeating after me, "Lord Jesus, I admit I have sinned both by commission and omission and I need your forgiveness. Thank you, thank you, that You paid the penalty for my sin when you died for me on the cross of Calvary. I accept Your way of salvation, and I ask you humbly to forgive me all my sin. I invite you into my life, and I ask you to be my Saviour and Lord. I surrender my life to You and ask You to help me follow and please You for the rest of my life. Thank you, Lord Jesus, Amen."

I could tell as I looked up into her face that she had met with Jesus Christ, and that He had accepted her, granting her His peace and joy! I showed her again 1 John 1:9 and said to her, "You confessed your sin to Jesus Christ, so, from this verse, what has happened to them?"

"He has forgiven me and cleansed me from all unrighteousness!"

"Wow!" I replied. "Isn't that absolutely wonderful! Now every time you become aware that you have sinned, please remember this wonderful promise and apply it in prayer again." I then turned to John 1:12 and said to her, "You received the Lord Jesus so what, from this verse, are you now?"

"I am now a child of God! And I feel like a new person!"

"Praise the Lord!" I said. "And now I want to show you John 10:27,28 – *'My sheep hear My voice, and I know them, and they follow Me. And I give them eternal life, and they shall never perish; neither shall anyone snatch them out of My hand.'* You have given your life to the Lord Jesus and promised with His help to follow Him...so what has He promised to give you?"

"Eternal life! And I shall never perish, and no one will snatch me from His hand!"

I went on to assure her that she was forgiven, a child of God, and assured of a home in heaven. I explained the basic need to read the Bible through, beginning with Matthew's Gospel and praying God would speak to her through His Word. "It may be in the first verse you read, or you may need to read five chapters before you really sense He is speaking to you." I explained the importance of daily prayer. "God is now your Father and He wants you to speak to Him about anything, anywhere, anytime!" I encouraged her to find a spiritual home and said that she was more than welcome to become a member of our family at Belvedere Christian Church. I encouraged her to phone her cousin, May with her wonderful news of becoming a Christian and to share her new found faith with others who may ask her. After a prayer for assurance and blessing, I committed Cybil into the Saviour's nail-scarred hands. She became a faithful member of our fellowship from then on.

One day Cybil phoned me to ask for prayer for her brother Bill. He was suffering from emphysema. He had been a heavy smoker all his adult life and was now paying the price. For a few days he had been in intensive care at the Avenues Clinic, and now the doctors had moved him into a private ward and requested his family to visit and say their last farewells. They predicted he would not last the day through. She told me that he was terrified of dying. I said that I would visit him and pray for him in person.

"Oh please, no," Cybil said. "He is not that way inclined!"

I knew that he had previously ridiculed Cybil for her new found faith, and now she was afraid that he would embarrass her by giving me the same treatment.

"Trust me, Cybil, I will ask God whether He would have me visit your brother, and should I believe He would then you know that I must go. Will you also pray for me? This may be his final opportunity to hear of God's love for him and God's desire to save him from a Christ-less eternity."

"OK, Pastor – I'll leave it up to you. God bless you!"

So I went. I asked at reception where Bill lay, found my way to his private ward, and upon entering the room found his family in a semi-circle around the foot of his bed. His wife Mavis was seated in a chair right up close to the head of his bed. I announced that I was Cybil's church minister, that Cybil had requested that I pray for her brother, and I asked if that was acceptable to them all. Mavis rose from her chair, moved aside, and with a very solemn tone thanked me for coming. She motioned to the chair she had vacated, and she took up a place next to the others at the foot of the bed. I sat down and introduced myself to Bill. His head was on the edge of the pillow, and he was facing me. In a very faint whisper that I instinctively moved my ear towards, he thanked me for coming.

"Are you afraid of dying?" I asked. This question was the first to come to mind, and although this was a novel approach (at least to me), and although I was surprised that I was asking such a forward question, I was acutely aware that he was dying, and time was fast running out. The Holy Spirit was giving me the words, and I really sensed His presence there.

"Yes I am!" he whispered back. "I'm terrified!"

"What you need is peace with God, and I am here to help you find it," I replied.

"Please go on," he whispered.

"The Bible says *'therefore being justified or declared righteous by faith, we have peace with God through our Lord Jesus Christ,'*" I continued. I took my diary out of my shirt pocket and placed it on the palm of my left hand. "Let this hand represent you, Bill, and let this diary represent a record of all the things you've done that you should not have done, and all the things you should have done that you have left undone." I paused to see that he had his eyes open, and he was watching my hands. "This record then represents a barrier that comes between you and a truly holy God." I pointed to the diary and then up into the air. "The Bible says that our sins have separated us from God. God, because of His great love for you, sent His Son, the Lord Jesus Christ, to this earth. So let this hand represent Jesus Christ (I showed him my right hand which I had raised above my head, and which I then brought down to the same level as my left hand). He never knew sin and so never had a barrier between Himself and His Father. Now the Bible says *'all we like sheep have gone astray; we have turned, every one, to His own way; and the Lord has laid on Him the iniquity of us all!'*" As I said the first half of this wonderfully moving verse I looked at and waved about my left hand with the diary on it. Then on reading the second half I moved that hand over to the right hand, tilted it and transferred the diary onto the right hand. I repeated it with an emotion I usually feel when using this powerful illustration. I looked intently at him to see whether "the light came on".

It did.

I could see that God was giving him the faith to believe!

"If you believe what I have shown you Bill, then you will be justified or declared righteous by your faith. God wants you to ask His forgiveness, which He promises to give you because of what Jesus Christ did for you on the cross. He also wants you to trust Him alone for your salvation by receiving Him into your heart and surrendering that heart to Him. In a simple prayer I can help you do just that. You will receive His peace and will not be afraid to die."

"I will need time to think about it!" he whispered back.

I could not believe what I was hearing.

He must have thought that I had not heard him, so he repeated what he had just whispered.

I panicked, thinking that time is just not what he had left. In the silence that followed, for I was speechless, I heard a voice in my heart. "Ask Me for time!"

I looked at that dying man with a mixture of compassion and respect. "Do you mind," I asked, "if I prayed for you that God would give you all the time you need to find peace with Him?"

"Certainly," he whispered back, "I would appreciate that."

So I poured out my heart to God. I reminded the Lord that He had sacrificed His life for Bill and I pleaded with Him that His sacrifice for him would not have been in vain. "May Bill be another trophy of Your amazing grace – please grant him all the time and faith he needs to make his peace with You! In the name of Jesus Christ my Lord, Amen."

Bill appeared moved by that prayer, as did his wife and family who had stood in silence throughout my time there. I took out from my top pocket a small orange tract called *The Four Spiritual Laws* and handed it over to Mavis. "Please read this to your husband," I asked politely. "God bless you. God bless you all!" I said as I left the room. I prayed quietly that God would use that tract not only to win Bill to Himself but also his dear wife.

Two days later I phoned Cybil. "I have not heard from you, Cybil," I began. "Please tell me about your brother."

"Ooh," she exclaimed. "I have been trying to get hold of you! There have been two miracles, Pastor, two miracles!" I could tell she was very excited.

"What are they?" I replied.

"Well the first is that my brother has been discharged from hospital and is back home!"

"Wow! That's wonderful Cybil. Now what is the second miracle?"

"The second miracle is that he is asking to see you!" She went on to apologise to me for trying to put me off seeing him and thanked me profusely for going anyway.

I was choked with emotion. "You told me to ask for more time Lord! I asked! You answered! Oh how I love You! What an adventure this is to serve You!"

I asked Cybil for her brother's phone number and address and immediately phoned for an appointment.

That afternoon I knocked on Bill and Mavis' front door. Mavis answered with a very warm greeting. She told me to make my way down the passage to the lounge, whilst she popped into her kitchen to put the kettle on. "My husband is sitting in his armchair, and we are very grateful to you for coming," she said.

Bill was sitting upright in his armchair. On the one arm of the chair sat the little orange *Four Spiritual Laws* tract. After thanking me for coming he lifted that tract in his right hand and waving it said, "There is a prayer in the back of this booklet, and my wife and I have been wondering whether we are allowed to pray it?"

Before I could answer he went on, "You see, pastor, I am seventy-seven years old now. I have lived all my life without God. I have been thinking that it is a real cheek for me to ask Him into my life now that I am dying!"

I think at that point my mouth dropped open! "Do you remember my prayer for you at the hospital?" I asked.

"How could I ever forget that prayer?" he replied.

"Do you remember how I asked the Lord to give you enough time and faith to find peace with Him?" I asked. "You were expected to die that day, weren't you?"

"Yes to both your questions," he said.

"If God thought it was a cheek for you to invite Him into your life now, then do you think He would not have let you die then? He has given you time – and He has given you faith. You may certainly say the sinner's prayer at the back of that booklet you are holding!"

Just then Mavis walked into the lounge. "Would you like milk and sugar with your tea, Pastor?" she asked, unaware of what had been said between her husband and I.

"Darling!" Bill exclaimed, "Pastor Henson says it's perfectly alright for us to say this prayer that's at the back of this booklet! Won't you pray it with me?"

"Certainly my darling!" she replied.

So I asked them to both bow their heads and pray the prayer after me. Each of us was in tears, and God's presence was awesome. Talk about trophies of grace! I was very emotional. I reassured them from Romans 5:1; 1 John 1:9; John 1:12; and John 10:27,28. I encouraged her to read God's Word to him, and I spoke of the privilege and wonder of prayer. I left that house on cloud nine!

Bill lived for another six months. During that time his wife read through the whole of the New Testament and quite a way through the Old Testament. He loved this Book of books. On my visits to him – he was not strong enough to attend the House of God – he loved discussing the Bible with me, and I often discussed what I had preached on the Sunday before. I learned that he had been a fighter pilot in World War II. Once he had had to ditch his plane whilst on convoy protection duty. He was rescued by the navy. Another time he had been shot down over France and managed to escape back to Britain. Later he had been shot down over Germany and had been taken prisoner to Stalag Luft North, the famous "Great Escape" POW Camp. He showed me his war log book that had German newspaper cuttings of articles where the Germans were denying shooting escaped POWs. He had chosen not to escape but rather sit out the war, as he had a wife and child back home to think about. Upon his return to Southern Rhodesia he began work at a large multi-national company where he had risen to become their chief accountant.

I was called to his bedside when he was dying again. It appeared to me to be the same private ward. The same family were gathered around – but this time his dying was so different. Even his family commented about the difference. He was not afraid. Thanks to God's saving grace through Jesus Christ, death had lost its sting and the grave had lost its victory!

I was asked to conduct Bill's funeral. It was held at the Warren Park Crematorium just outside Harare, and the chapel was jam-packed with mourners, with many standing both inside and out. And I was, by God's grace and with enormous privilege, able to give the testimony of how he came to find peace with God and so inherit eternal life.

Chapter 6

He Made it up to Them
Paul's Story

M ary and two of her eight children came to our church one Sunday morning service. I greeted them at the door. Mary told me that she lived nearby and was just looking for a church for herself and a Sunday school for Ian and Alice. I welcomed her saying that we have the children in with us for the first half hour of worship. I pointed to my wife Clare who was quietly playing the keyboard by the platform and told her that Clare would take the children out through the back of the church to the vestry where she would teach them Sunday school. "I pray that you will all feel at home here and will enjoy our service," I said as Mary gently laid her hands on each child's shoulder to lead them to their seats.

I always become both excited and slightly anxious when new people come to church. I believe it is true to say that I sense a heightened awareness of God's holy presence when those seeking Him find their way into His house. I do not know whether I had heard it from another preacher or it came as a revelation or observation to me, but I firmly believe that the Lord Jesus, the Great Shepherd, is keener to rescue the lost sheep than tend to the ninety nine who are safe. So I have told my congregations that if I perceive there is anyone in the congregation who is not in Christ's kingdom, I will preach a Gospel message to teach them how to enter, even if I have to drop what I had prepared. I do not want anyone on judgement day to say to the Lord, "I went to Belvedere Christian Church, Christian Life Centre or Oasis Christian Centre and they never told me how to become a Christian!"

So that Sunday when I preached I modified what I had prepared to include the simple Gospel message of the lengths Jesus Christ went to to make a meaningful and personal relationship with Him possible. At the close of the sermon I said, "Let us bow our heads in prayer," and I proceeded to ask the Lord to help us believe what had been preached and to put it all into practice.

"Whilst all our heads are bowed and all our eyes are closed," I continued, "I appeal to anyone here who has not yet received Jesus Christ into your life to cleanse you from your sin, to save you from the consequences of that sin – to be your Saviour; I appeal to any of you who still occupy the throne of your own life but now want to surrender that throne to Jesus Christ – to be your Lord and Friend; I appeal to any of you who really want to become a true Christian to now raise your one hand."

To my great joy, Mary shot up her right hand and lifted her head, opened for a moment her eyes to see if I had seen, then bowed her head again and lowered her hand.

"I see that hand," I said. "Is there anyone else?"

No one else responded and I did not wait long before I said, "I am going to pray a prayer which I ask the one who raised their hand to pray with me – just quietly but with your heart. If anyone else here did not raise their hand but would like to pray the sinner's prayer, please would you also pray after me. 'Lord Jesus, I believe You love me enough to take my sin and be punished in my place. I am so sorry for my sin – I turn my back on the way I have been living and ask You to please forgive me. I invite You into my life to be my Saviour and Lord. I give the rest of my life to You. I want to live it for You. I thank You that You have forgiven me now according to Your promise. Thank You too that You have now made me Your child and given me Your life – eternal life. Please help me follow You all my life. In Jesus' name, Amen.'"

I then asked to see anyone who had said that prayer. I explained that I needed to show them from the Bible the assurance that they have experienced a genuine conversion. Mary was indeed the only one to respond, but I could see from her countenance that she had had a glorious encounter with the Lord Jesus Himself. The Sunday school had filed out of the vestry by now so she could explain to her two children that she would be a few minutes talking to Clare and me in the vestry. As they were five and eight years old and were a little shy, they came back in with us and sat quietly on the floor nearby.

I opened my Bible at Acts 3:19, pointed to the verse for Mary to read with me, and read, "'*Repent therefore and be converted, that your sins may be blotted out, so that times of refreshing may come from the presence of the Lord*'. You have repented Mary in that you have expressed sorrow about your sin, and you have turned your back on the way you have been living without God – so from this verse, what can you say has happened to your sins?"

"They have been blotted out!" she said, her face beaming with joy and peace.

"Wonderful beyond words!" I replied, "That means that God has given you a brand new start – your slate is wiped clean! Now Mary, the Bible does warn us that we will be tempted to sin throughout our lives. Should we fall for any temptation there is a verse in 1 John 1:9, '*If we confess our sins, He is faithful and just to forgive us our sins and to cleanse us from all unrighteousness.*' Every time you sin you need to ask God's forgiveness and then believe in His willingness to cleanse you afresh."

"Mary," I continued. "You also invited the Lord Jesus into your life as your Saviour and Lord, didn't you?"

"Yes, I did!"

"Then let us read this verse in Revelation 3:20, '*Behold, I stand at the door and knock. If anyone hears My voice and opens the door, I will come in to him and dine with him, and he with Me.'* From this verse, Mary, where is the Lord Jesus right now?"

"In my heart!" came her delighted reply.

"Just when you thought it could not get any better you need to look at this verse," I said as I turned to John 1:12, "*'But as many as received Him, to them He gave the right to become children of God, to those who believe in His name.'* What is God's Word here telling you that you have become?"

"A child of God. I am a child of God!" she exclaimed, "You hear that, Ian and Alice? I am a child of God. I am a true Christian!" The children leapt up from off the floor, and Mary embraced them both. God had given their mother an experience of a lifetime. They had probably never seen her as ecstatic as this before.

"There is more," I interrupted. "Read with me John 5:24, *'Most assuredly, I say to you, he who hears My word and believes in Him who sent Me has everlasting life, and shall not come into judgment, but has passed from death into life.'* From this wonderful verse, Mary, please tell me what you now possess and what you will not have to face?"

"I have everlasting life, and I will not come into judgment!" I could see that it was almost too much to take in at once. This was better news to her than if she had heard that she had won all the lotteries in the world!

In her own beautiful way, Clare reached over and gave Mary a hug. "Welcome," she said, "Welcome into God's wonderful family. We are now sisters. God is our Father!"

I asked Clare to pray that God would seal everything He had said to Mary in her heart and so give Mary complete assurance that she was now His and He was now hers. We encouraged her to talk to God about everything, anywhere and anytime. We encouraged her to prayerfully read God's Word, beginning at Matthew's Gospel, and to read until she senses God is speaking to her heart. "It may take just one verse or you may read five chapters before you hear from Him in your heart," we said. We encouraged her to gather with other Christians, whether it was with us at the Belvedere Christian Centre or at another one of God's fine churches in Harare.

Mary stood to her feet, bent over her children to whisper in their ears to thank Clare for their Sunday school lesson, and took them by the hand to walk home. Clare and I looked into each other's eyes, embraced each other and felt deeply that this was one of the crowning joys of being in the Lord's service.

Mary, Ian and Alice never missed a meeting if they could help it. A few weeks after her conversion, I had the privilege of baptising Mary. Immediately after her baptism we prayed for her to receive the baptism of the Holy Spirit. Ian and Alice soon developed a personal relationship with the Lord Jesus through Clare's teaching at Sunday school and their mother's example and teaching at home.

I did endeavour to win Mary's husband Paul to Christ, but to no avail. He was just not interested. He was happy for Mary, Ian and Alice to pursue their new-found faith, but he told me to leave him alone to live his life the way he wanted to live it.

After one Sunday morning service Mary called Clare and I aside to express her deep concerns for her husband. "You already know that he is a heavy drinker," she began. "What you do not know yet is that when he has had too many he often resorts to four-dollar-a-night prostitutes." She paused to see our reaction to this shocking news before asking, "Does God expect me to be a 'proper wife' to him, knowing the probability he may contract HIV Aids from them?"

I looked immediately at Clare thinking she would have a good answer, but the look on her face told me that Mary wanted the answer both from her Pastor and from a man. It was my responsibility, and I believed that God would impart His wisdom through me to His precious child. "I believe that before God, Ian and Alice are your prime responsibility. You need to do all that you can to protect yourself for their sakes. We are so saddened that this has been happening, and we will be praying for you all!"

I do not remember how long after that conversation I received a phone call from Mary. It may have been a year or even two years. "Pastor John," she began in a tone of voice that told me of bad news to come. "Paul is in a private ward at the Pariwenatwa Hospital. He has been there for over two weeks. I know that I should have told you before now for you to at least pray for him. To be honest with you, I have enjoyed the break from him and his drunken behaviour."

"What is the diagnosis, Mary?" I asked.

"It's very bad, Pastor. First his kidneys failed so they put him onto one of their dialysis machines. When they first did that they tested his blood for HIV." She fell silent for a few seconds. I knew then what was coming. "Well, they have the results back, and he is HIV positive. So they have refused him any more dialysis treatment, to prevent contamination of their machines I suppose. Pastor, Paul is dying, and I do not know what to do!" and she began to cry. Despite Paul's abusive treatment of his wife and children, she still loved and cared for him.

"You tell me where Paul's private ward is, and I will go and visit him," I replied.

She told me but then added, "Pastor, the hospital called me in this morning to take a blood sample from me to test me for the HIV virus. Please pray for me! It will be a miracle if I do not have it too!"

I felt like I had been hit in the solar plexus. My heart screamed out a denial. "Mary, you have really honoured the Lord, so I will believe with you that the tests will come back negative. When will you have the results?"

"I was told it would be two weeks, and I am sure it will be the longest two weeks of my life," she said.

As soon as Paul recognised me that afternoon, he began to cry. He waved with his arms but remained speechless. He kept shaking his head and then bowing it. I sensed that after all his previous rejections of me and the Gospel I had tried to share with him, he just could not believe that I had not written him off as a hopeless case. There I stood beside his bed as an ambassador of the Lord Jesus Christ. The Lord Jesus had not written him off!

I sat down in the chair beside his bed. Paul was a lapsed Roman Catholic, so he was familiar with the confessional. He knew now that I had sat down to listen to him and to talk to him. Before I could begin to talk to him, he began his long confession. I listened in silence. I asked no questions. I patiently looked into his eyes. Sometimes he closed them. Sometimes he looked away in shame and self-loathing. I imagined early on in his confession the Lord God laying those same sins on His own beloved Son during those three dark hours on the cross. On account of his and mankind's sins Christ had cried out, *"My God, My God, why have You forsaken Me?"*

Paul spoke of his rebellion against God and His church; of his severe neglect and abuse of wife and children; of his adulteries with friends and prostitutes; of his lying and cheating, greed and selfish exploitations and manipulations; of his drunkenness and licentiousness. He had seared his conscience, and he believed he deserved to contract HIV, to have kidney failure, and to be tormented forever in hell.

Finally Paul reached out for my hands which I freely offered him and clasping them tight he asked, "Pastor John, is there any hope for me?"

"Only if you place all your faith in what I am about to demonstrate to you," I began. "Let this diary of mine..." (I removed my diary from my shirt pocket and waved it before him) "represent a record of all your sins of commission and omission." I paused and then asked, "A better illustration would be a much larger diary, wouldn't it, Paul?"

"Yes, I agree," he replied sincerely, "A much larger diary!" I had felt it important not to minimize the quantity of his sin, for he certainly had not.

Pointing with my right hand, first to my left hand and then to the ceiling, I continued, "Say this hand represents you and God is up here. Then the

Bible says, *'Behold, the Lord's hand is not shortened, that it cannot save; nor His ear heavy, that it cannot hear. But your iniquities have separated you from your God; and your sins have hidden His face from you, so that He will not hear.'* As I was quoting these verses I was placing the diary onto my left hand. "This record of your sin forms an impenetrable barrier between you and a truly holy God. The only solution to this huge problem was for God to come to earth Himself in the Person of His Son Jesus Christ." I raised my right hand and brought it down to the same level as the left hand with the diary on it. Then looking at my right hand I said, "The Lord Jesus was tempted in every way that we are, yet He never sinned. He had no barrier whatever between Himself and His Father. Now the Bible says, *'All we like sheep have gone astray; We have turned, every one, to his own way; and the Lord has laid on Him the iniquity of us all.'*" As I said the second half of the verse, I brought my left hand across to the right hand and turned the diary over into the palm of my right hand.

After repeating this illustration twice more I said, "Paul, your only hope for the forgiveness of your sin is to believe that because Jesus Christ paid in full the penalty of your sin, God is both willing and able to forgive you all your sin. There is no way you can save yourself. Jesus Christ is your one and only Saviour. He is your only hope. By repenting – and by that I mean telling God how very sorry you are for your rebellion and sin and turning your back on that way of life to go God's way instead, God promises forgiveness, and you make Christ's death in your place worthwhile. What is more, Paul, if you invite the Lord Jesus into your life to clean you up and take charge, He has promised to accept your invitation, and in return He will adopt you as His own child and give you eternal life. You will no longer be afraid to die, and Mary and the kids will no longer be afraid that you are lost to them forever. Would you like me to pray for you?"

"Yes! Yes please!" he replied. I could see that he understood Christ's simple and most wonderful Gospel of grace. The Holy Spirit was about His wonderful work. So I prayed that God would grant him the repentance and faith to receive His forgiveness and peace. I then led him in the "sinner's prayer", and to my indescribable joy I witnessed the great transaction between Saviour and sinner. Paul was born again. He was a new creation. Christ had received another reward for His sacrifice on that old rugged cross.

I opened the Gideon's Bible that was in his bedside cupboard, and I read with him the wonderful verses of assurance from Acts 3:19, Revelations 3:20; John 1:12 and John 5:24. When I prayed the prayer for God to seal everything in Paul's heart and to give him complete assurance of his salvation, I had an overwhelming sense that God wanted to prolong his life to make things up to his family. "Please, dear Lord," I prayed, "Grant to Paul enough time to makes things up to his wife and children."

I encouraged Paul to pray. "Faith stands for 'Father All In Thy Hands', Paul. To exercise faith you need to put everyone and everything into God's nail-scarred hands. Whilst you are here in hospital you will find plenty of time to do that, and it will make a world of difference to you and to them."

I handed him the Gideon's Bible and went to the pages that give Scripture readings for all kinds of needs and questions. I encouraged him to read what grabbed his attention, and I also asked him to read systematically and prayerfully through John's Gospel. "You will get a great deal of assurance from John's Gospel. What you do not understand, you can ask me when I return to visit you," I added.

Finally, I asked him to break the news to his dear wife when she visited him later that afternoon. "She has prayed so much for this day," I said "And she will be over the moon with joy to hear of your conversion. So will your children!" I shook his hand warmly, and he smiled broadly. He was so different, and Jesus Christ had made that difference. Only He could!

Mary phoned me the moment she returned home from visiting Paul that afternoon. She was so excited and thankful that she could hardly contain herself. "He asked my forgiveness for all the years of abuse and neglect he had put me and the children through. He told me that he believed that God had forgiven him and with great emotion he gave me that illustration you so often use of God laying on the Lord Jesus the sin of us all. We cried and cried together. I feel God has healed our marriage! I worship Him, Pastor John. I give Him all the glory for His mercy and grace! Hallelujah!"

"Clare and I are just so happy for you, Mary! God has answered your prayers! By the way, did Paul tell you about my prayer for him?" I asked.

"You mean your prayer that God would give him enough time to make it up to me and our children?"

"Yes, that prayer!"

"We would so love it if God answered that prayer. I feel that we have fallen in love with each other all over again, although this time it is so different. God has done it!"

Paul's kidneys began working again, and he was moved to a private hospital for a further two weeks before he was released to return home. During that time I visited him regularly, and we discussed not only how to walk with the Lord in the light of His Word, but also how best he could make it up to his family for all those wasted years.

It was also during the second week that Mary had her blood test results back. To the enormous relief of Mary, Clare, myself, and perhaps, especially, Paul, the results were negative. Miraculously, it would seem, Mary had not acquired the dreaded HIV from Paul.

Paul's health declined rapidly some six months later, and he passed on to be with the Lord he now so loved. I conducted his funeral. His one daughter flew back from London, where she had been pursuing a singing career. His older five sons were there as were Ian and Alice. They all either shook my hands warmly or hugged me. They all thanked me for giving their father back to them! In the six months God had extended his life, Paul had dated his children for the first time in their lives. He had taken them out to meals and for ice-creams; he had bought them shoes and clothes and special gifts; he had loved them!

Mary was especially grateful for those six months with her "brand new husband". He had been to their solicitor to draw up his first will; he had sorted out all his paperwork and finance; he had taught Mary how to run his business that had run down somewhat prior to and during his illness; he had walled their property for her security and peace of mind; he had redecorated their home and built a new living room onto it; he had bought new furniture with her and surprised her with the purchase of a good second hand Mercedes Benz. He had dated her and romanced her. "God answered your prayer, Pastor John! He made it up to us!" she said as she embraced both Clare and I.

At the reception after the funeral, Mary called me aside and said, "I have inherited the business, Pastor John. I feel out of my depth. Can you advise me what to do now?"

"Mary, you know that I am not a business man, so I would also be out of my depth," I replied honestly but not with a discouraging manner. "What I can advise you to do is hand the whole business over to the Lord Jesus, just as you have your life. That will mean instating Him as your Senior Partner. Always go to Him in prayer before you make any decision. Ask Him for wisdom throughout the day. Do not allow for others to get you into a corner or manipulate you into making quick decisions. Tell them you need to consult your Senior Partner first. As the Bible says, 'Let the peace of God rule in your heart.' In other words, Mary, 'If in doubt, don't!' Don't be afraid to ask advice from those who know what they are doing. Your foreman has been in the company a long time. He will help you I am sure. Just let him and your other employees know Who now owns the business. Let them know that He is your Senior Partner."

"I will remember all that," said Mary. "Thank you, Pastor John. You have given me some really good advice." She fell silent for a few moments before she said resolutely, "I will do just what you have advised me to do. Thank you!"

The following week Mary phoned me, "I have just been to see our Solicitor, Pastor John, and I took my Senior Partner with me. It is all going to be alright." I think that she had assumed that she had told me what she needed to see him for. I did not ask her any details, and I congratulated her for her wonderful attitude.

"God will bless you, Mary," I replied. "He will look after you and the children well. He has promised in His Word that He would be the husband to the widow and the father to the fatherless. He will also be a brilliant Senior Partner, and His business will prosper. He will prove Himself to be true to His promises, I guarantee that!"

A month or two later Mary told me that she had really "got into the swing of running a business with God at the helm." She had caught up on the backlog and was ready for growth. "I have asked my Boss to bring in more work, so watch this space," she concluded.

Every Sunday Mary was placing a sizeable cheque in our tithe box. Her monthly tithe was at least half the total tithe coming in. I had never mentioned tithing to her, and we had a policy in our church to not take offerings nor ask publicly for money. We had a box at the entrance to the church, and we prayed the finance in. The Lord Jesus watched over that box, and what came in was a matter between Him and the donor. What Mary was giving was a huge blessing to us, so one Sunday I told her so. "I am tithing from the business," she said, "My Senior Partner asked me to."

A few days later she phoned and excitedly said, "We have just received a massive order from the Zimbabwe government. I told them we were up to the work but would need a considerable increase in our foreign currency allocation to fulfil the order. Our allocations had been £10,000 every six months and guess what?" "What?" I replied.

"The government has promised to increase our foreign currency allocation to £10,000 every month. That is a six-fold increase, Pastor! Isn't God so good?"

"Very good, Mary. God is always very good!"

Chapter 7

An Amazing Miracle
Brian's Story

As soon as Michael went in to the nursery-school classroom his Christian teacher called me aside to tell me about Michael's friend's father. "Something terrible has happened to Stevie's dad," she began. "He was hit across the back yesterday, and he is now at the Pariwenatwa hospital paralyzed from his chest down. Will you please go and visit him and pray for him? I am not sure if he is a Christian. He is in ward B, ground floor, and his name is Brian. Visiting hours are from three till six."

"I'll visit him at eleven this morning. As a minister I have visiting rights anytime," I said.

I found Brian in a private ward and in a miserable state. He was very pleased to see me and said that his son Stevie had told him all about my son Michael. He then told me what had happened to him.

"I am, or should I say, I was the financial controller of a big furniture factory. We had sold $700,000 worth of furniture to Zambia and have not been paid for it. So we had high level talks in the company about recouping the costs. The conclusion was to shed some of our factory workers. The workforce rioted, and they believed that I was somehow to blame. So they ordered me out of my office, prevented me from taking my company car, and ordered me to leave the factory. As I neared the gates some b...... whacked me across the back with a pole. I very quickly slumped to the ground, paralyzed. I am expecting, very shortly, the neurologist and the neurosurgeon to come in to give me the diagnosis and prognosis."

Having bravely told me this much, Brian became overcome with emotion and began to cry.

"I feel so desperately sorry for you, Brian. This is a complete tragedy!" I replied.

"Listen to this," he said through his crying. "My wife saw me here last night, and she announced that I was no longer any good to her and she was leaving me. She will be taking the children too! So I have literally lost everything – my health, my job and with that no doubt my home, and now my wife and children!"

"What you need, Brian, is a miracle!" I found myself saying as I was struck by the sheer scale of this tragedy.

"You are certainly right there!" was his reply.

"Do you mind if I pray for that right now?" I asked.

"Sure!" he said as he closed his eyes.

Just then the door opened, and in walked the neurologist and the neurosurgeon. I stood up and promised Brian that I would be back when they left. I then introduced myself to them and politely left the room, closing the door behind me. I must have waited for at least half an hour whilst those specialists ran tests on Brian and discussed with him both his condition and his future treatment.

When they left I went back in. Brian was again very emotional. "Not good news," I said, reading his body language.

"Those specialists were in here for a long time. I did not expect you to hang around for so long."

"Well, I promised to pray for you. So what's the story?" I asked.

"They told me that I have nerves that have been severed, and they will never be restored. It looks like I am paralyzed for life! Tomorrow morning at eleven I'll be having a colostomy so as to get my bowels emptied." He paused and shook his head in despair. "I cannot believe this is happening to me! You said I needed a miracle. You were absolutely right!"

"You also need a personal relationship with Jesus Christ. Whether He heals you or not, you need Him to be with you for the rest of your life's journey. Have you asked Him to forgive your past, and have you invited Him to be your Saviour and Lord? Have you placed your whole life into His hands?"

"No, but I can see that I do need Him. Would you help me to know Him personally – like you obviously do?" he asked.

I told Brian all about the cross of Calvary, about the suffering Messiah, and how He suffered for our salvation. I took him to Isaiah 53:6 and did my illustration of God laying on Jesus Christ the iniquity of us all. I could see that God gave him the faith to believe in Christ's atoning work. He wanted to repent of his past and receive Christ into his life to be his Saviour and Lord. We prayed together the "sinner's prayer" and Brian began his new life with Christ.

I was overwhelmed at all that was happening. God was clearly at work and I sensed both Brian and I were ready to pray for the physical miracle he so sorely needed. I not only prayed for complete recovery of his spinal injury and all his nerves – what amounted to a creative miracle – but that God would perform this miracle in time to prevent the colostomy. When I left Brian that afternoon he was in a hopeful mood and seemed to have a real peace.

I visited Brian the next afternoon. He was on his own. As soon as he saw me he smiled broadly. "My bowels worked! My bowels worked!" he exclaimed as I reached out my hand to shake his. He was so excited, like as if he had inherited millions.

"Tell me about it!" I said excitedly.

"Remember I told you that I had been scheduled to have the colostomy at eleven this morning?" he asked and then, before I could answer, he continued, "My bowels worked at ten, and I no longer need a colostomy! God has started the miracle!"

For the next hour we talked about God's goodness, faithfulness, and love. We ended our time with praise and a prayer that God would restore his marriage and take care of his family and finances.

Brian slowly began to get feeling back in his one side. Soon he was placed in St Giles Rehabilitation Centre where he received intensive physiotherapy. One day, in front of a cheering crowd of fellow patients, Brian took his first steps. He was aided by a special three-pronged walking stick as his one side was still limp and useless. He began to drive again and to attend our church.

After one Sunday service he asked for prayer, and my assistant-pastor, Deon and I prayed for him. He needed a job – and quickly, as he had huge financial needs. He had bought his smallholding where he lived using a Deed of Sale agreement, and the sellers were taking him to court because he was behind on payments. He could lose his home if God did not come through for him. Whilst he was very grateful that he could drive and get about, he still needed the completion of the miracle of healing. He also wanted his marriage and family restored.

I had previously encouraged Brian not to sign any divorce papers served on him by his wife, but when he was in his garden one day and the courier arrived with the papers, he signed them. He later told me that he had been depressed that day and in his weakness had signed them, regretting it as soon as the courier left his property.

Deon asked God specifically that Brian would have an excellent job by Friday. That following Sunday Brian announced that he had been offered an excellent job starting that Monday. The following week when he went to court over his property, the court allowed him the time to catch up on his payments, and so his home was secured.

Sadly his wife was not interested in returning to live with "a cripple", but did allow the children to visit him at weekends. In fact, she eloped with a younger man and, within months, married him. When that young man was called up to do military service in South Africa, she realized she had made a huge mistake, and she told Brian this over a meal at a restaurant. He was overjoyed and still prayed that she would return to him. She dashed those hopes when she eloped with another younger man. I advised Brian that according to Scripture there was now no hope of him remarrying her, and that he ought to look to God for someone special who would love him regardless of his infirmity.

Brian was given books on how to secure his total healing, and when asked "how are you?" his standard reply became "I am completely healed!" I was very disturbed by this denial of obvious facts, and one Sunday God led me to preach on Divine Healing. In the sermon I explained, with Bible references, that healing was a sovereign act of Almighty God. There was no formula. Sometimes God responded to the person's faith, sometimes to the faith of the person's friends, sometimes He healed when there was little faith, and sometimes, as in the case of the raising of Lazarus from the dead, He exercised His own faith.

In the Old Testament God called Himself *"The Lord that heals you"* and in the New Testament Peter says *"Jesus the Christ heals you!"* I explained that some He healed by His Word or command; others by His touch; some by casting out devils, and others after their obedience to His instructions. He could heal directly or indirectly through medication and the medical profession. He also left us believers with the instruction to cast out devils, lay hands on the sick, anoint with oil in His Name, and pray for the sick. When we are sick we are to call for the elders for the anointing of oil and prayer. When the elders come, we are not to deny we are sick but confess it and receive prayer. Ultimately we must *"look to Jesus, the Author and Finisher of our faith"*.

I called forward anyone who wanted prayer, and Brian dragged himself to the front and sat down on a front seat. When Deon and I reached him he was weeping. His shoulders were shaking with emotion.

"What would you like prayer for?" I asked him.

"I need to repent!" was his emotional response.

"Repent for what, Brian?" I asked, knowing that he was already a committed Christian.

"Repent of trying to heal myself instead of looking to Jesus and trusting Him for my healing!" he said, looking up to see our reaction. I had not said those words in my sermon yet he had interpreted his "positive confession" of healing as an attempt on his part to heal himself.

I then gathered the congregation around Brian, and together we called on God to complete the healing of Brian's broken body. There was an awesome sense of God's presence in that time of prayer, even though Brian returned to his seat the same way as he had come.

That night I was preaching in a small village some fifteen miles away from Harare. Deon was taking the service back in Harare, and Clare was there to play the piano. To the complete delight of all attending that service, Brian arrived walking perfectly normally, and without his special walking stick. God had honoured his repentance and our heartfelt prayers. God had confirmed His Word! Deon called him to the front to give his testimony.

Closing his eyes and raising his arms horizontally, Brian explained that he would certainly have fallen over if he had tried this co-ordination test before his healing. Then he walked up and down, jumped up and down and raising His hands towards heaven shouted, "I am healed! God Himself has done it! Hallelujah!" The congregation went wild with excitement. They honestly thought that revival had come. Clare could hardly contain her joy as she related to me the events of that Sunday evening service.

I phoned Brian as soon as I had heard the story from Clare. "My miracle is complete! God has done it all! Hallelujah!" he exclaimed. "What I did not tell you this morning was that I was discharged from Saint Giles on Friday. I was given a final assessment and was told that there was nothing more that physiotherapy or medical science could do for me. I would have to learn to live with my disability. That is one of the reasons why I was so emotional this morning." He paused and then said, "So you are right John – man's extremities are God's opportunities!"

"May I suggest that you return to Saint Giles and ask for another assessment, Brian? It would be to the glory of God if your miracle healing is verified by the medical profession," I said excitedly.

"That is exactly what I planned to do," he replied. "I will do that just as soon as I can get time off work, and I will get back to you with the results."

The next evening Brian phoned. "I know that this is your day off, John, but I just could not wait to tell you the great news. I went to see Lawrence, my physiotherapist, and demanded from him another assessment. I say demanded because at first request he refused, saying that he had given me my final assessment and was not prepared to give me another. I then closed the door and said that I would not leave his office until he had run some tests on me that would prove I had been miraculously healed. Well you know John, as he was doing these tests his little Indian eyes were getting bigger and bigger and he kept shaking his head. He then conceded that I was indeed one hundred percent healed. So there you have it John! Verified! Oh, by the way, he asked about our church and promised to come this Sunday!"

Lawrence did come to church as promised. After the service I talked with him. He told me that he came from South India where he and his wife had studied at a Methodist Medical Mission. His wife was a trained nurse, and they had come over to Zimbabwe for a two year period. She was doing a shift at Saint Giles, but he would encourage her to come to our church the next Sunday. He confirmed to me that God had obviously healed Brian. He described the healing as miraculous. I asked him whether he would be prepared to testify to the miracle when he came the next Sunday. He was delighted with the invitation, and the following Sunday, flanked by his wife, he bore witness to God's healing touch on Brian.

Brian, soon after his healing, began to court a beautiful lady from work. She proved to be an ideal match for him and months later I had the enormous privilege of conducting their wedding. It proved to be the answer to the final need he expressed when I first met him.

Later Brian joined our worship team and every year, on the anniversary of his dramatic healing, he had the congregation sing:

"Something beautiful, something good,
All my confusion He understood.
All I had to offer Him was brokenness and strife,
And He made something beautiful of my life."

Chapter 8

Profound Comfort
Anne's Story

"Good afternoon," I said in my usual cheerful manner as I answered the phone one April afternoon.

"Pastor John!" was the reply. "I have very bad news…" Then she went silent.

"Is that you Anne?" I asked.

"Yes, it's me…, Oh Pastor John… David died this afternoon. He fell down the mine shaft…," She fell silent again as the full force of her news hit my heart and tore it apart. Clare and I loved David. He had recently planned to take early retirement from the mine so that he could be a full-time elder in our growing church. We loved Anne just as much.

"Anne, this is unbelievable news!" I said as I tried to put myself together again and be her pastor and comforter. "Would you like Clare and I to come out to you right away? We will quickly organize a baby-sitter for the boys so that we can spend as long as you like out there with you."

"Pastor John… you have no idea how much that will mean to me. I have phoned my son, Joe in South Africa, and he will be contacting the rest of the family. As you already know, I have no family left here in Zimbabwe – except of course my church family. Joe promised to be here by tomorrow evening." She was beginning to compose herself, but I knew how very close she was to her husband, and I knew that her whole world had been turned upside down and inside out.

"Let me pray for you over the phone, Anne. The Bible calls God the God of all comfort, and I pray, Lord, that You wrap Your everlasting and ever-loving arms around Anne and hold her close to Your heart. I pray that You comfort her in her gigantic loss! Your love dictates that You weep with those who weep. You are well acquainted with grief. Comfort all the family and all David's friends and associates we pray, in Jesus' Name, Amen."

As soon as we could, Clare and I were travelling the forty miles to the mine that had been David's home and workplace for some five years. He was the mine captain. Each weekend he and Anne had spent in the static caravan a couple of miles from our church. They both loved God sincerely, and they loved the church family too. We wondered how best to break the awful news to the church. We reminisced about the wonderful times of fellowship we had enjoyed with them both.

Anne was David's second wife. David had a son by his previous wife, and Anne also had children by a previous husband. Not long into their marriage they began to have regrets and the marriage was in jeopardy. That was when they sought out a church for help. There they found the Lord Jesus Christ and were very soundly converted. This turned their marriage around and the whole time we knew them we witnessed a model marriage. They left us in no doubt that they adored one another.

Shortly after their conversion, David and Anne actively sought ways to serve the Lord. He wanted to go to Bible College and become a pastor or evangelist. He applied but was turned down on the grounds that he was still a very young Christian and because he was a divorcee. Then one day he came across an alcoholic with three young children. They were living in abject poverty and squalor. David felt compelled to foster those children and on returning home he announced to Anne that he now knew how they could serve the Lord Jesus. They could foster children and raise them to love and serve the Lord. Those three children were their first foster children. They went on to foster, over the years, sixteen more children. At the time of his tragic death, David and Anne were looking after two teenagers.

We spent hours with Anne that evening. There were times when she wept, and we wept with her. Then she would remember something funny, and we would laugh with her. We were all on a roller coaster of emotions. She could not believe that David could have accidentally fallen down the mineshaft. The thought that he could have been pushed was equally repugnant. What the witnesses did tell her was that David's only words whilst falling were, "Jesus, Jesus, Jesus!" He loved that precious Name! Anglo American, the multinational that owned the mine, was sending safety investigators to assess the situation on the mine and give a detailed report.

Anne also told us the remarkable story of the holiday that they had returned from only a week ago. David had been on a mission. He wanted to see every relative of his throughout Southern Africa. On their way home he had insisted on visiting his estranged son in Bulawayo. The estrangement had begun when David left this son's mother some twenty years before. Anne announced with real pride that David had been fully reconciled to him, and that that had greatly relieved and delighted him. "It is almost as though David had a premonition that God was calling him home, and that he needed to tie up all the loose ends beforehand," she concluded.

"God has a thousand ways to comfort us, Anne, and that could certainly be one of them," I said. I was reminded of how my own father had wanted to take early retirement in order to go to Bible College with me and train for full-time ministry. He went to serve the Lord in heaven just two weeks before Clare and I left for Bible College.

I will never forget David's funeral. The mine hired a large bus to bring in the mineworkers. The church was packed. Anglo American sent two representatives, and the church family turned out in force. Anne insisted on the coffin being open and once the service began I led her from the back of the church to the front where the coffin stood. She leaned over and kissed David's lifeless face, and then she sat down as the congregation formed an orderly line to pass the coffin and peer in. As part of my eulogy I read from the Anglo American magazine that described David as a gentle giant. They acknowledged his strong Christian faith and resultant high integrity. They also said that the mine he captained was the best run and safest of all their operations in Southern Africa. They too mourned his loss.

Clare and I went out to Anne's home at the mine for the reception after the service. All her family were there and it was good to catch up with them all. Anne knew that she would have to vacate the house within the week to make way for the new mine captain. Persuaded by her family, she announced that she would be moving to her mobile home whilst all her affairs were set in order, and then she would move to Durban in South Africa to be near Joe and his family. We expected but regretted that news.

Anne had a very nervous disposition. As a consequence, she suffered from stomach ulcers. These flared up during the trauma of her loss, and now they were bleeding. An appointment was made with the specialist who wanted to use an endoscope to see whether it was now time to do invasive surgery to remove them. Whilst waiting for the appointment Anne invited us to her static caravan for a cup of tea.

"How much does the church owe on its mortgage?" Anne asked as she poured out the tea.

"Why do you want to know?" I asked, perplexed.

"I have been a member of your church for the past five years, and so I believe that I have a right to know!" she said with a cheeky tone and smile.

"As a matter of fact," I said, "The latest mortgage statement came this morning, and I can tell you exactly how much is owed."

Anne excused herself "for a moment" once I had given her the figure, and a couple of minutes later she returned with a cheque for the full amount. It was an awful lot of money. I feebly protested, but she countered me by saying, "The insurance has paid up and I received considerably more than that. I have been so blessed at the church and under your ministry, and I feel that to clear the church's debt is the least that I could do. I also believe that David would have wanted me to do it!"

I was overwhelmed. At the beginning of the year I had specifically asked God to clear our mortgage debt. I offered to take Anne to the surgery to see the specialist the following week. She declined saying she needed to learn to fend for herself, and that with God's help she was sure to be alright.

It was a huge weight off my mind when I deposited Anne's cheque the next morning. When we left Harare the following year we left the church with a very healthy bank balance. Praise the Lord.

The following week, Anne phoned. "I have changed my mind about going to see the specialist," she began. "I am in such a state about my health that I do not think I could cope, especially with the drive home after the examination. So please could I take you up on your offer to take me and fetch me?"

"Certainly, Anne," I replied.

In the car park before she climbed out of my car I offered to pray for her. I could see that she was terrified. I wanted God to calm her down and give her His peace. I also desperately wanted Him to heal her. She had endured enough as it was, and the prospect of invasive surgery seemed so very unfair. Fresh in my mind was the fact that she had cleared the church debt. She had done that with no other motives than to thank God for His goodness to her and to bless His church.

"Lord Jesus," I prayed, "Please calm Anne with your perfect peace. Give her the conviction that she is your precious daughter and that You have her in Your nail-scarred hands. Please, Lord, heal her completely." To my surprise I finished my prayer with, "And when the specialist goes in with his endoscope may he find nothing there! In Your name I pray this, Amen."

I walked Anne to the reception and, as there was no waiting room, I told her I would wait for her out in my car. I had my Bible to read, so I was content.

About half an hour later, Anne emerged from the surgery. I left the car to meet her. She was in tears and my first fear was that she had bad news. Seeing me she rushed up to me and gave me a big hug. "I am completely healed," she said with high emotion, "God has completely healed me, Pastor John!"

As we walked back to the car, she told me of how the specialist wiggled the endoscope around and said, "I cannot find the blasted things!" He then turned the monitor around so that he could show her the inside of her stomach. "You see those pin-pricks," he continued, pointing on the monitor, "I think that those are the last of them. I cannot explain it, but you are completely healed!" She burst into tears out of sheer relief. Her tears were tears of joy and not of sorrow. I cried too. Then we laughed for joy!

Anne left for South Africa about a month later. Joe had flown up so that he could drive her down. We were very sad to say goodbye, and we promised to keep in touch.

A month later I received a letter from her. She wanted me to know that when God healed her of her ulcers, He also healed her of her nervous disposition. Before she left the mine three months before, I had a special steering lock and an alarm fitted to her Peugeot 504 car. This was because she was petrified that it would be stolen when she moved to Harare or to South Africa. She told me that her son and daughter-in-law had collected her to take her to the theatre. Before climbing into their car, she had gone to her car to collect something. The theatre had begun when she looked for sweets in her handbag and discovered that her large bunch of keys was missing. Instantly she knew that they must still be in the door of her car that was parked in an open car park outside the block of flats where she lived. Before her healing, she wrote, she would have panicked and then insisted that her son race back to her car to see whether it was still there. Now that she was healed, she calmly put the whole matter into God's hands and enjoyed the theatre. When they finally returned to her home, she discovered that her bunch of keys, which included her flat key, was still in the door of her car. She gave all praise and glory to God.

Chapter 9

Dealing with an Alcoholic
Andrew's Story

The telephone rang one evening. "My name is Andrew Andrews," announced the caller in a broad Scottish accent. My first thought was that it was Stuart, a real fun guy from our church, calling and trying to wind me up. He was superb at taking off other accents, and I could just not believe that any parent would give their child the name Andrew Andrews. I thought though that I would play along with him.

"Good evening, Andrew! How can I help?" I replied.

"I am an alcoholic who has just become a Christian, and I have been told that you are a good pastor and would look after me."

"Could you please tell me who referred you to me?" I enquired.

"Jonathan Pringle," came the reply.

I knew Jonathan well, and he too was a practical joker. Now I was convinced that Stuart was impersonating this man so I said, "Come on Stuart, stop having me on!"

To my deep embarrassment, Andrew ignored my comment and proceeded to tell me that he was moving to Horsham from Storrington where he had been led to the Lord by an elderly couple after a run-in with the police. He asked to see me and we met up for the first time at my church office the next day.

Andrew had been sober for about three months. He was estranged from his wife Mary and was looking for accommodation in Horsham. He asked for prayer that his application with the council for a house or flat would be successful. He was also facing a court hearing as he was under probation from Worthing and needed to come under a new probation order for Horsham. He asked for prayer about that as his current probation officer was very harsh and unsympathetic to him and his "illness". He told me about his alcohol addiction and how he had ended up in a homeless shelter in Storrington. Whilst there, he had come off alcohol simply because he had run out of money to buy any more. No one would lend or give him money either. The forced withdrawal had sent him into an alcoholic fit. During that fit he had bitten through his tongue, and another resident had called for the ambulance. He told me how he resisted going in the ambulance because, despite bleeding profusely from his mouth, he desperately wanted another drink!

It was in the ambulance that Andrew called on God for mercy. He was stitched up and sobered up and when he returned to Storrington, he went along to the local evangelical church. There he met with an elderly Christian couple who not only led him to pray the sinner's prayer, but also took him under their wing to mentor him. He soon gave his testimony in that church, and that is when he met Jonathan. When they heard that he was hoping to move to Horsham to be closer to his wife and to look for work, they recommended he be mentored by me and attend Christian Life Centre.

I was thrilled to hear his testimony. I told him a bit about myself and the Christian Life Centre before praying for him. I prayed not only for his accommodation needs, his impending court hearing, and his work opportunity, but also for a full reconciliation with his wife and family. As I shook his hand I felt I had made a good friend, and we would be on a journey together. We arranged to see each other after the court hearing.

Andrew had an amazing testimony when we next met. His Worthing probation officer had been unable to attend the court hearing, and his deputy had displayed a completely different attitude. He had met up with Andrew before the hearing to get to know him. He had been undoubtedly impressed that Andrew had experienced a radical change in his life. In court he managed to convince the Magistrate that Andrew had served his probation and that no further supervision would be necessary! Then Andrew went around to Horsham District Council's housing department, and they had a one bed-roomed, furnished, semi-detached home waiting for him. Within the week he was employed too.

Andrew joined the Horsham Alcoholics Anonymous where he boldly shared his new-found faith. "The Higher Power," he told those who were gathered in a circle in the Quakers Meeting House, "Is none other than the Lord Jesus Christ. I know now because I have met Him and invited Him into my life to be my Lord and Saviour!"

His confession of faith was met each time with frostiness and, from the leader of the meeting, with open hostility. This greatly frustrated Andrew, but he felt called to help those tormented by the addiction that he had now been freed from. He met up with other alcoholics in the evenings or at weekends, and he sought to persuade them to turn to Jesus Christ for help.

I do not know what triggered a relapse into alcohol abuse. Perhaps it was conditions at his work where he was very overqualified for the job. He did tell me of his frustrations there. Perhaps it was the bond that he felt with the alcoholics he was trying to help. Perhaps it was simply the pay check and a voice inside his head that said, "You really deserve a drink". Perhaps it was because Mary was still not interested in reconciliation, and his son and daughter still wanted nothing more to do with him.

The relapse lasted about two months. He lost his job. I would visit him in his little home where I would plead with him to see drink as his enemy, not his friend. "With every step you take towards the off-licence, Andrew, you have a choice. God says, '*I have set before you life and death, blessing and cursing. Therefore choose life!*'"

He tried to explain to me that it was an illness, and that he had no control over it. If he stopped he could have an alcoholic fit and that could prove fatal. He would have to slowly cut down and so avoid the hallucinations and the tremors. He displayed great frustration with me when I insisted that what he needed to learn is the little word "No!" I told him that he should be man enough to endure the withdrawal symptoms. I knew enough about alcoholics to know that they were practically powerless to "cut back slowly" – because one sip of alcohol always led to more.

"You just do not understand," he would say over and over again. He was right of course. I did not understand in the way he meant. The first time that I ever drank alcohol was shortly after my conversion when I was attending a wedding in Salisbury, Rhodesia. One sip of the Champagne went straight to my head and made me feel giddy. Another sip and I felt nauseous. I did not finish the glass! Shortly after that I read in the Bible that John the Baptist *"Will be great in the sight of the Lord, and shall drink neither wine nor strong drink. He will also be filled with the Holy Spirit."* I determined then that I too would never drink alcohol. I must add here that I know of many fine Christians who do not share this conviction, and I do not have a problem with that.

When I began as a new pastor, I visited a lady who apologized for not taking communion during our communion services. I asked her why since the Lord Jesus commanded *"Drink from it, all of you."*

"Oh," she said, "I am an alcoholic and one sip of the communion wine could set me off on the downward slippery slope again."

"The wine we use in the communion is non-alcoholic," I assured her. "It is grape-juice! Since it symbolizes the sinless blood of Christ, it has to be non-alcoholic!"

"Are you sure of that?" she asked excitedly.

"Absolutely sure!" I assured her.

She proceeded to tell me that she had begun to drink heavily to kill the monotony of her life. She was not happily married and would drink secretly to hide the habit from her husband and to help her lose her inhibitions with him. She had been free now for a few years, and she attributed the victory over the addiction to her encounter with the Lord Jesus. He was now her closest friend and alcohol was her most bitter enemy.

I did understand that some people could drink heavily at weekends and yet never become addicted. Others drink moderately and something happens that turns their brains into an alcohol dependency so that they become addicted. They have to avoid alcohol at all costs to save them from ruin. I have read of a preacher's teetotal father who was coerced to have just one glass of wine at a Christmas office party, and he was instantly addicted and remained so for twenty-five years. That story still scares me!

One day when I visited Andrew I managed to persuade him to let me have the patio key, "Just in case you cannot come to the door," I said. That was when he appeared to be so very weak that I thought he could easily pass out or even pass away. There were cans of Tennents Extra Strong beer strewn across the floor. He had messed the sofa and the carpet. The smell assaulted my sinuses. My offer to take him to the hospital was turned down. I pleaded with him to stop. I prayed with him to stop. I pleaded with God to deliver him. I commanded the devil to leave him. I reached the end of my rope, and he finally promised me he would quit.

"You can see the state I am in, John," he said. "I could not possibly walk the mile to the off-licence to replenish my stock. I could never persuade you to even get me two cans to help me come down. I am finished!" He picked up the telephone and dialed his doctor. The receptionist knew him well and gave him an appointment for the next morning. I promised to take him there. He still had a couple of cans to see him through the night so after a warm handshake from me I left.

I fetched Andrew the next morning. He seemed very docile and compliant. He regretted the trouble he was putting me to, and he made repeated promises to get back on to the straight and narrow. His face was puffy and red, his clothes dishevelled, and his speech slow. He was unshaven, and he smelled. What a

difference to the first time I met up with him. He had taken real pride in his appearance then.

I waited with him in the surgery waiting room. He asked me to come in with him to meet his doctor. I said that I had never before done such a thing, but he insisted, saying that the doctor and I were part of the same team to ensure his recovery. When he was called, he asked the doctor whether I could join him, and the doctor very willingly obliged. After patiently listening to his story, during which he heaped praise on me for all the help I'd been to him, the doctor asked him to lie on the bed where he prodded around his abdomen, just beneath his ribcage.

"Your liver is distended and probably damaged by your alcohol input. We'll need to put you on vitamin B complex to help repair that damage. I'll also prescribe something to stabilize you and help you come down from your alcohol high. It will reduce the hallucinations and tremors and prevent you taking another fit. You will however have to promise me that you will not have any alcohol whilst on this medication. That would prove very dangerous and may be fatal."

"You know I hate making promises doctor," said Andrew as he climbed off the bed and put his shirt and jumper back on. "But I am determined, really determined to give up drinking. With yours and John's help…and God's, we'll beat this thing!"

I collected his prescriptions from the neighbouring pharmacy, and we headed back to his place in a positive mood. I had purchase bottled water for him so that he could take the first dosage on the way back. Although I offered to help clean up the horrendous mess in his home, he said I had done enough and that he needed to do it all himself.

The following day I visited Andrew. He had not cleaned up, and he had more beer cans around his armchair. I was bitterly disappointed, even angry. I took the remaining cans and poured the contents down the kitchen sink. He promised he would take his medication. He also assured me that he was in no state to walk the mile to the nearest off-licence to buy more drink. He wanted me to leave him alone, and so I left.

I went on to visit one of our elderly members nearby and about an hour and a half later began my journey back to the church office. As I travelled down the Old Crawley Road, to my utter amazement, I saw Andrew striding on the footpath in the opposite direction. Clasped firmly in his one hand was a large plastic bag full of beer cans. I stopped my car and chased after him on foot. When he saw me he stopped dead in his tracks, he slumped his shoulders in resignation, and angrily said, "So you caught me in the act!"

"What on earth are you up to, Andrew?" I asked impatiently. "You promised me you would start your medication, and you told me you were in no state to be able to manage the walk to the off-licence. Where did you get the strength to walk all the way there?"

"You really don't understand alcoholics, John!" he said. "When a person who has this disease needs a fix, he will be prepared to crawl on hands and knees over broken glass for miles to get it!"

"You need food, not drink, so please hand me that bag. I will get a refund and spend that on some decent food for you. You carry on home, and I'll meet you there as soon as I can."

By now Andrew knew I meant business, and he meekly handed me the bag and silently turned to head slowly back to his house. I took the bag to the off-licence where I described Andrew and asked on his behalf for a refund. The shop assistant obviously had never before had such a request, so he went into his manager's office to ask advice.

When he returned he said, "I am sorry sir, we cannot help you. If you had bought these cans then we would be obliged to refund you on your request. Since Mr Andrews bought them, he will have to come in himself for his own refund."

I flushed with anger. "You sold alcohol to a man who was, by his appearance, obviously an alcoholic. What you do not know is that he is on medication which, if taken with alcohol, could kill him. Having aided him in his degradation, are you prepared to have his death on your conscience? I will open each one of these cans and empty them right outside your door. I will not return them to Mr Andrews! I intended to spend the refund on some decent food for him, because I am out to save his life and not destroy it!"

I grabbed the bag from off the counter and was about to storm out of the shop when the assistant stopped me. His face had paled through this altercation, and he meekly went to his till and withdrew the refund. I took a deep breath to calm down. I thanked him and went to the neighbouring store to buy Andrew food and fruit juice.

Andrew recovered. He shaved, cleaned himself and his home up, and he had his hair cut before setting out to find another job. I was thrilled when he found one and was positive about his future. I also contacted his wife Mary and spent some time hearing her story.

For years, she told me, she had put up with his alcohol abuse. She would clean him up and put him to bed when he came home drunk at night. The next morning she would often phone up his work to give an excuse for him not being able to go in. He was never violent when drunk. Alcohol loosened his tongue and she would have to put up with endless ramblings. Alcohol also made him exceedingly self-centred and self-obsessed. He became deceitful and paranoid. She really suffered. What eventually persuaded her to ask him to leave home was the discovery of £100 cheques on their bank statements which he refused to account for. She investigated and discovered that they were for the services of prostitutes. It was that discovery and disclosure to their daughter that turned her from a sweet devoted daughter into someone who never wanted to have anything more to do with him.

Mary promised me that if Andrew was sober for Christmas, she would be happy to have him come for a family Christmas dinner. I was thrilled, and so was Andrew. I was aware that he had to take one day at a time, and that his sobriety was not guaranteed. But it was a great goal to work towards.

I think it was his finding out that his daughter would not be coming to the family Christmas dinner if he came that started the next bout of alcohol abuse. When I visited him to find the beer cans scattered around his armchair and him in a drunken stupor, his daughter's rejection of him was his main topic of conversation. His son and daughter-in-law would be at the dinner, and I told him that that was progress and well worth fighting for. Eventually I persuaded him to seek medical help, and the next morning I was back with him at his doctor's surgery.

On returning to his home, Andrew insisted on cleaning up again, and he gave me strong assurances that he would be in church on Christmas Day and, if I did not mind, I could take him to his wife's home for the Christmas dinner. I prayed with him and left praying for God to have mercy on him and his family.

I do not normally buy Christmas presents for congregation members, but I felt to buy Andrew a small box of Scottish shortbread. I wrapped it in Christmas paper and took it to church. He did not come. I felt gutted. At the end of the service, I asked Clare, if she did not mind, to return home with our sons and niece whilst I visited Andrew. Alan overheard me and asked if he could join me. He would come up after me in his own car.

I arrived at Andrew's front door and pressed the door-bell. No response. I pressed it again. There was still no response. I tried to convince myself that his son had called for him and he had gone to his wife's home already. But a terrible fear settled over me, and I rushed around to let myself in via the patio doors. I still had the key. I was hit by the stench. The lounge was a mess. Beer cans were strewn all over the carpet. There was a smell of stale urine and vomit. I rushed through to his bedroom where the smell almost overwhelmed me.

Andrew was lying on the floor next to his bed. His face, arms and feet were a deathly grey colour. He had his pyjamas on but he had vomited down the front and been incontinent down his legs. I was gagging with the smell. I bent down to hold his throat to feel his pulse. There was one. I could also feel air coming from his nostrils, and there was a slight gurgling sound coming from his mouth which was open and dribbling. I quickly surveyed the floor. There was a broken glass jar near his one hand. Scattered around it were a few tablets. That bottle had been full two days before when I'd taken him to the doctor. Had he overdosed? He had certainly disobeyed his doctor's strong instruction not to drink whilst on those tablets.

Just then the door-bell rang.

I left Andrew and rushed to the door. There stood Alan. "Have you got your mobile phone, Alan?" was my greeting.

"No!" he replied. "What's going on?" I was keeping him at the door, not wanting him to see down the passageway into the bedroom. Alan's father had been a Royal Marine who had also succumbed to alcohol abuse. As a young teenager Alan had to visit his father in a sanatorium where he eventually died from liver disease. I did not want him to see Andrew in a similar state. Just then the smell hit Alan, and he gasped as his hand swung up to his nose to block it.

"Andrew is in a very bad way," I hurriedly said. "He has not only been drinking but I am sure he has overdosed on his medication. Could you please go around to Beryl's and call for an ambulance?"

Without saying another word Alan rushed to his car and sped off. My immediate thought was to clean Andrew up. It was Christmas day, and I felt so strongly that no ambulance crew should have to be assaulted by that smell. So I rushed into the bathroom and ran the bath. There was a bottle of bubble bath on the shelf, and I emptied it under the taps. I then went through to Andrew's bedroom where I grabbed him by the shoulders and dragged him through to the bathroom. He was still unconscious and therefore a dead weight. He left a slimy trail behind him. I undressed him and manhandled him over the side of the bath.

As I set to work soaping him down through the bubbles, Andrew was incontinent again. My heart sank. Instinctively, it seems, I drained the bath out and refilled it. Now I was in a panic. Would I have him ready in time for the ambulance? By the time I began manhandling Andrew out of the bath and on to a towel, he began to come around from his coma. I dragged him through to a dry part of the passageway where I proceeded to dress him in clean clothes I found in his wardrobe.

I had just laid Andrew's head on a cushion when the two ambulance crew arrived at the door with Alan behind them. I gave them a brief history of his alcoholism, and I collected up the medicine bottle so the doctors would know what he had overdosed on. One of the crew went back into the ambulance to collect a wheelchair, and then they both lifted Andrew into it. Just then Andrew turned to me and began to mumble something.

I could not catch what he was trying to say so I said, "Andrew, please speak up. I cannot hear what you are trying to tell me." He mumbled again but with an earnest look on his face. I still could not understand him. The crew was now ready to load him into the ambulance, and I could see they were eager to leave so I stood back and stared.

Alan came up besides me, and as I turned to speak to him, I was overcome with emotion. "He said his last words to me Alan, and I do not know what they were!" He put his arm around me and assured me that I had done all I could.

"You go on down to your sister's now Alan. I need to do a couple of things in the house before I return home." He reluctantly left me to go back into that house. I took bleach and tried to clean the mess in the carpets. It just did not seem to work, so I ripped up those carpets, wrapped cling film around them and took them to the outside large bin. His pyjamas, towels, sheets and blankets I stuffed into the washing machine. I loaded it with the maximum amount of detergent and turned the temperature setting to 65 degrees centigrade. I seemed obsessed to not inflict that smell on the neighbours either side of his home. I took my shoes off and thoroughly cleaned them in bleach.

When I climbed in to my car, I had a splitting headache. I phoned Mary as soon as I returned home to find that she was not at all surprised. She phoned the hospital before phoning me back to say that they had given him a stomach pump, and that he was in a critical condition. She was devastated but very grateful for my help. By the tone of her voice it appeared to me that she did not hold out much hope for his recovery.

But recover he did! Mary phoned me on Boxing Day to inform me that Andrew had pulled through. Her son would be giving her a lift to see Andrew in the hospital that afternoon. I offered to meet them there.

Andrew was now in a general ward but still hooked up to intravenous feeds. His face was very puffy and a mixture of red and blue. He was still very weak and struggled to stay awake. He thanked me for being there for him and proceeded to tell us that the doctors had said that if he had been found just an hour later he would have died. He acknowledged that he was alive only by the grace of God. He had not intended to end his own life but rather escape its realities. He kept apologizing for the trouble he had put us all through, and he kept assuring us, by God's grace that he would never drink again.

I was not sure when last Andrew had seen his wife or his son. He was clearly both pleased and embarrassed to see them again. His conversation with us exhausted him, and so we withdrew to a waiting room after only twenty minutes. There I had the opportunity of speaking to Andrew's son Gary for the first time. He was very grateful to me for saving his dad's life, but at the same time he was perplexed about my involvement with him. Gary loved his father despite everything. It would have been his worst nightmare to have gone around to Andrew's house to find him dead on the floor. Mary was grief stricken, and she kept saying, "I just cannot understand him! He was doing so well and had been looking forward to Christmas dinner with us!"

Andrew remained in hospital until January 2. He returned to his house and cleaned it thoroughly. He now took a job stacking shelves in a big supermarket. He told me that it was menial work but carried little stress, and he worked with friendly people. He soon became their code-checker, and after a short time boasted that he was the best code-checker in the south. He attended church faithfully and we were firm friends once more. I would meet him for coffee once a week before the start of his shift.

After a few months Mary booked a holiday in Greece for them both. She had set him a goal, and we were all thrilled that he remained sober until and through the two weeks they were away together. He fully expected Mary to invite him back into their family home, but when she refused, he went back to drinking. This time I discovered a Roman Catholic rehab place in Northern Ireland that would take him in on a donations basis. I booked his ticket and took him, worse for wear, to the airport. I hung about in departures afraid he would not be allowed on board because he could barely hold a straight line. But he made it.

Six weeks later Andrew phoned me. He was home. He asked for prayer that the supermarket would give him back his job. They did. Over coffee he told me how wonderful the rehab place was. He sobered up over a week there and was soon serving at admissions. His jobs were to welcome new inmates, show them the facilities, bath or shower them, and then settle them in, sometimes holding their hands as they went through detox. He saw some men come for two or three days and then leave for more heavy drinking before returning again. It made him face up to how very degrading alcohol abuse can be. He wanted now to devote his life to helping alcoholics recover. He rejoined the local Alcoholics Anonymous.

Andrew began meeting up with Mary regularly. After some months the Housing Department of the local council offered to pay him a lump sum if he would vacate his home. This amount would clear Mary's mortgage and so the decision was made. Andrew moved back into the family home. As soon as he did I made him promise two things. First that he would move out the minute he began drinking again, and second that his wages would go into a joint account where she had to sign for every withdrawal. He agreed.

Months later Mary phoned to say, "I am so sorry to have to tell you this John, but Andrew has started drinking again."

I could hear him in the background shouting abuse at Mary. He did not want me to know. Why she had phoned anyway was because he had pushed her around, and she saw that as the beginnings of violence toward her. He had in the past been verbally abusive when drunk. This was the first time he had become physically abusive. She was scared.

I rushed around to their house. Mary met me at the door. She looked petrified! Just then Andrew began to shout at Mary. I rushed into the lounge where I saw him in his armchair with an almost empty large bottle of brandy. I sat down opposite him to tell him calmly that he had broken his promise to Mary, so that I would have to remove him from the house. Mary told me that he must have stolen the brandy from Waitrose Supermarket. I promised to go there the next day to warn them to keep an eye on him. I would also go to Marks and Spencers in case he tried to steal from them too. That made him rant and rave. Remaining as calm as I could, I attempted to lift him up off his chair. He brushed me aside as he stood up.

"I am going to my bed to sleep this off," he said as he attempted to brush me aside again.

"No, you are not!" I said firmly. "You are coming with me!"

He then pushed me back and began swearing at Mary. As he took hold of the banister to begin his climb up the stairs to his room, I grabbed his arm and said, "You are coming with me, Andrew!"

"Where?" he retorted as he made an attempt to break free. I tightened my grip and pulled him toward the front door. He took a swing at Mary who was standing in the passageway in tears. I flushed with anger, swung around the back of him, and grabbing him under both armpits, I manhandled him out the front door. Once out he relaxed and meekly went with me to the car. I had an old towel in the car, and I placed it on the passenger seat to spare it from his incontinence. He complied and sat there, while I rushed around to the driver's side to start up before he made a bolt for it.

"Where are you taking me?" he asked. I realized not only that I still had not answered his previous question, but that I did not have a clue.

"I do not know yet, Andrew, but it will be where there is no chance of you returning to Mary tonight."

When I reached the roundabout I felt led to head for Worthing, some twenty miles away. He complained about my cruelty for a while, and I reminded him of the conditions he had agreed to when moving back with Mary. We then sat in solemn silence.

As I approached the Storrington roundabout I remembered that he was familiar with the town and would know where to lay his head for the night. So I swung in to Storrington, explaining to Andrew my plan. There was no public transport from Storrington to Horsham at that time of night, and he would have to rough it until morning. I dropped him off in the middle of town and headed back home. I arrived back at about 11.30pm and fell sound asleep. I was exhausted.

At 2.30am the phone rang. It woke me from a deep sleep, and it took me a while to orientate myself.

"My name is PC Irvine from Storrington Police Station. I have with me a Mr Andrew Andrews. He told me that you had dumped him here in the middle of Storrington. He made his way to Mr and Mrs Martin, elderly residents here, and there is no way they can cope with him in his condition. What do you think you were doing dumping him here?"

"I am very sorry that Andrew made his way to the Martins. I honestly did not think that that would happen," I said, trying to get my wits about me. "I took him from his home because I judged him to be a danger to his wife. I could not take him to the hospital, as I know they would not have a bed for him. I took him to Storrington believing that he knew where to sleep rough there as he had lived there prior to coming to Horsham. The police in Horsham would have not been able to do anything unless he had actually assaulted his wife. I would therefore like you to tell me what solution you would have come up with had you been in my place."

Whilst I was talking I could hear Andrew talking in the background. PC Irvine was obviously listening to us both. He calmed down and said, "Mr Andrews is now telling me that you are a very good man, that you have saved his life on at least one occasion, and that he does not want me to accuse you of anything. I am sorry that I came down on you so hard. I do believe that I would have done something similar to what you have done, and I applaud you for helping this man so much in the past. We cannot put him in one of our police cells, but we will take him to Pulborough Railway Station where he can sleep on a bench and return by train to Horsham in the morning. I have a blanket here that I can give him. I apologize for troubling you at this hour of the morning."

Mary phoned me at midday the next day to say that Andrew was home. He was in the bath which is always a good sign, and she was very grateful indeed for the rather radical steps I had taken to protect her. She had cleaned up all his mess and was hoping that his experience had taught him that there were severe consequences to his wrong choices. She had told him that next time he falls off the wagon, she would not have him back.

Andrew recovered. The supermarket had him back to work. We were friends again. Shortly after this recovery, Gary announced that Andrew was going to be a grandfather. Andrew could not contain his excitement. This made him even more determined to stay off alcohol. It also heightened his appreciation of God's grace in saving him.

At the time of writing, Andrew is sober. His granddaughter has become the light of his life. She adores him, and they often either have her at weekends or else they travel to Oxford to spend weekends with her there. Andrew reads her bed-time Bible stories which she loves. She has now begun primary schooling.

His favourite Psalm was Psalm 40 which goes like this:

I waited patiently and expectantly for the Lord;
and He inclined to me, and heard my cry.
He also brought me up out of a horrible pit
 a pit of tumult and of destruction,
Out of the miry clay (froth and slime),
And set my feet upon a rock,
And established my steps.
He has put a new song in my mouth
Praise to our God;
Many will see it and fear,
And will trust in the Lord.

Many have wondered why I spent so much time and effort with Andrew. I have two reasons. The first has to do with the value he is to God Himself. God so loves him that He gave up His only begotten Son for him. Having created him God had also redeemed him. I did not want Christ's sacrifice for him on Calvary's cross to have been in vain. The second reason comes in the sincere answer to the question that governs my life here – "What would Jesus do?" Although there were many times when I felt like throwing in the towel, there were no times when I felt that God had given up on him.

Chapter 10

Won by God's Presence
Matt and Pearl's Story

I believe their story began with a very special prayer meeting. We had just completed the ground floor work on our church building. It all looked so very new, light and inviting. As I walked through the main hall to the back hall where we were to pray, Ian said to me, "The old has gone, John. It is actually really hard to remember how this building looked when we first began work on it." He stopped walking and so did I. "I believe God wants to make us new too," he continued. "To do that, I believe we need to say sorry to God for our past."

He looked at the puzzled look on my face before explaining, "Several people like Peter and Jane have been really wounded here in this church. They have been so wounded that they have vowed to never return here. I believe that although none of us coming to this prayer meeting are responsible for that, God was grieved by it, and we need to apologize to Him."

I agreed with him. I sensed that God had put these thoughts on Ian's heart. When our prayer meeting began I spoke of Daniel repenting on behalf of his nation as though their sin was his sin. I also spoke of how the Lord Jesus said that if we wanted to be great in His kingdom we needed to remain as little children. "A distinguishing feature about little children is they have no past. They only have a future. As they grow to adulthood they build up a past. Some of that past is bad and some good. It is the bad that God wants to forgive or heal."

I asked Ian to share with the group what he had shared with me, and we went straight into prayer. "We are so very sorry, Lord, that people like Peter and Jane have been so wounded in this church. We acknowledge that it grieved You, and we are so sorry!"

The presence of God filled that back room, and soon we were all in tears. We became very emotional as we keenly felt God's grief for everything unkind that had been said and done in His church and in His Name. As we closed the meeting, we felt there had been a spiritual breakthrough. God was making us new.

The following week Peter walked into the church to inspect all the changes to the building. I met him and immediately told him about that prayer meeting where we had said sorry to God.

"I want to say sorry to you on behalf of the church here, and I humbly ask for your forgiveness," I concluded.

Peter's eyes filled with tears, and without saying a word he wrapped his arms around me and gave me a big hug. It was a holy time. He released me and then excitedly asked about the building plan. I had the joy of showing him around the building, and he left a happy man. Two days later he phoned me.

"Jane and I have been discussing where we could hold our fortieth wedding anniversary party. We have both agreed to ask you whether we could hold it in your church."

"We would be overjoyed to have your party here!" I replied. What a wonderful breakthrough!

Whilst praying for them the next week I felt it laid upon my heart to ask Peter to preach the day after the party. He was delighted, and I shall never forget his sermon. He preached about bearing the marks of our Lord Jesus. He then held out his right hand and described how, as a child, he had gashed his hand wide open. It bled a lot, and he had to have several stitches to seal the wound, anti-biotic to stem the infection, and anti-tetanus serum to prevent tetanus. After several days the wound had healed, and he was pain-free. Since then he has borne the scar but been free of the pain. With regard to the wounds inflicted by others prior to his leaving the church, they had all healed, and he only has a scar to remind him. He related his wounding at the hands of a few church members and declared that it no longer hurt. All was forgiven and he was pain-free.

Within a couple of weeks Ian phoned me really upset, "My daughter, Louise is in deep distress. She is willing to see you, but is too shy to phone you herself. Please phone her and go and see her." He told me enough to go on, and I phoned her and made an appointment to see her.

Louise acknowledged that distancing herself from the Saviour she had once loved had brought troubles on her. I spoke to her about the parable of the prodigal son. She knew the story well and was overjoyed to realize that the Father welcomed her home with open arms and a forgiving heart. She recommitted her heart to the Lord Jesus. Then she said, "I really am very serious about living for the Lord Jesus from now on. To show that to my family and friends, I would like to be baptized again."

I was overjoyed. I felt like I was attending the party the Father was throwing on her behalf. So I did a Bible study on baptism in water and in the Holy Spirit, and we set a date. I phoned her just before her baptism to confirm that she was well up for it. I gave her advice on the sharing of her testimony, and I let her know how privileged I felt to be baptizing her. It was then that she told me that she had invited her business partner and his wife to her baptism. "They are not Christians," she told me, "So please pray for them."

I greeted Matt and Pearl as they nervously came through the front doors. "We have come for Louise's baptism," said Matt as he scanned the church to see where she was.

"Louise is sitting with her parents in the front row," I said, pointing to her. "There are two seats next to her. Perhaps you would like to sit there."

"Thank you," Matt replied somewhat coolly. He took Pearl by the arm and marched up to the front, sitting next to Louise immediately in front of the baptistry.

Justine led the worship, and Matt and Pearl were amazed at how sure she was in her faith. By what she said and the way she sang she demonstrated a heartfelt love of her Saviour. Nevertheless, both Matt and Pearl were very uncomfortable, so much so that Louise sensed it and whispered to them that they were free to just sit and listen if they wanted. So they sat down and tried to settle down too. They soon abandoned thoughts of walking out. Their physical discomfort also disappeared.

That was when the band started the third song, "Open the eyes of my heart, Lord, Open the eyes of my heart, I want to see You, I want to see You." The Lord made His presence known to them, and they both began to cry. Clare and I were standing right behind them, and we saw them both wiping away their tears.

I preached on the Parable of the Prodigal Son from a Jewish perspective. I related a couple of stories of Jewish friends at university. Had I known that Matt's mother was Jewish (a Levite even), I probably would not have been so confident about my message. During my message, I mentioned "repentance", and Matt thought, "See, there's that Christian word 'repentance'. That's the kind of thing that puts me off. It makes me think of crazy people on the street shouting, 'Repent!' What does repentance mean anyway?"

Just then Matt saw me stop mid-sentence, like I had received "a download from heaven", and I turned towards him and said, "And for those of you who don't know what 'repentance' is, it is simply you are going your own way with your life, and you stop and do a 180 and go God's way instead."

This "spooked him"! The Lord had his attention!

Louise gave a wonderful testimony, and then I went into the water with Louise's dad to baptize her. It was a very moving experience, and when I looked up I noticed Pearl crying and Matt holding back his tears.

Over coffee and tea I spoke to them, "I see that you have been deeply moved by the service. Can I be of any help to you?"

"There is a presence here," said Pearl.

"That is the presence of the Lord," I replied.

"Oh!" she replied.

I went up to my office and returned with a copy of *The Cross and the Switchblade*. I told them that it is a great read, and I was sure they would get a lot out of it.

Then I called Louise, her parents, and Clare to my office to pray for Louise for the Baptism in the Holy Spirit and the gift of speaking in an unknown language – what I affectionately call the Holy Spirit's prayer language. To my surprise and consternation, Matt and Pearl followed us up to the office, found seats for themselves and joined in the meeting. Having given Louise a few Scriptures on what to expect, I offered to pray for her. She looked furtively at Matt and Pearl and sensing her discomfort with their presence, I swallowed hard and politely asked them to wait for Louise downstairs. They felt rejected!

They had been intrigued by the supernatural and felt a desire for it themselves, even though they were not yet "born again".

In the car on the way home, Pearl told Matt she felt that she had finally found what she had been searching for all her life. In her "New Age" lifestyle, she had believed she'd been communicating with angels. But who better to be her spiritual guide than the master, Jesus Himself! Since Matt had a strong distaste for the name "Jesus," he was not too pleased that she felt that she had found Jesus. The rest of the thirty-five mile journey home was spent in silence.

However, all that week Matt was deep in thought. He admitted to himself that he knew nothing about God or Christianity. He could not deny having encountered God's presence in the meeting and concluded that God was indeed real, and He was trying to reach him. He decided to give God a chance, and he picked up *The Cross and the Switchblade* that I had given them, and he read it through. He was fascinated at the supernatural experiences described in that wonderful book, and he began to crave the supernatural experience of knowing God for himself. Matt and Pearl did not discuss the subject. Well, not until that Saturday night.

"So, you want to go to church tomorrow?" he asked as they relaxed together on their couch.

"Yeah!" Pearl replied.

They went to bed early that night. They giggled at the thought of their outrageous decision. On the way back to Horsham the next morning their conversation was interrupted every now and then with an exclamation, "I can't believe that we're going to CHURCH!"

Our congregation very warmly received them, and they soon settled down to enjoying the service. A colleague of mine was preaching, since Clare and I were celebrating our twenty-fifth wedding anniversary in Guernsey that weekend. God continued to speak to their hearts, and the following Sunday they were back, hungry for more. I preached a gospel message and gave a short appeal for converts at the close. Although there was no response to my appeal, Pearl invited me at the end of the service to come to Louise's that afternoon to speak to her about how to become a Christian. Louise had invited her and Matt for lunch.

Upon my arrival, Pearl ushered me immediately into Louise's lounge. Louise and Matt remained in the dining room.

"I want to know Jesus Christ for myself," she began. "I realized two weeks ago that He is what I have been searching for all my life! I found Him in your church. Please help me to relate to Him."

"Let me begin by telling you a fictitious story," I replied. "There was a young woman who visited a large department store. It had everything in it from groceries to furniture, from pharmaceuticals to electrical appliances. At the entrance to the store a man offered her a store credit card. 'You will never need to bring cash into this store,' he promised her. 'You'll be able to buy absolutely anything you want using this store card.'

"She signed for the card, and within days she received it in the post. During the months that followed she ran up a huge debt. When she failed to pay the monthly minimum, she was called by the store's credit controller. 'We have made a decision to withdraw your store card and to require that you pay us all that you owe.'

"'There is no way that I could ever pay you what I owe. Won't you have mercy on me and forgive me?' she pleaded.

"'Certainly not!' he said emphatically. 'Just imagine if we were to forgive everyone their debts – we would soon enough be bankrupt. If we do not have the money by Friday you will receive a court summons, and we will see you in court.'

"Since she simply cannot pay, she duly receives a summons to appear in court in a few months time. Whilst she is anxiously awaiting her trial, she falls in love with a young man. She keeps her debt as a secret from him until two nights before the court case. On that night, at a romantic restaurant, he asks her to marry him. 'Oh how I would love to say *yes*!' she exclaims, 'But, in two days time I am due to appear in court over a huge debt I owe the department store. As there is no way that I can afford to pay, I am sure to be sentenced to prison. It is just not possible to say yes to you!'

"The young man accompanies her to the court. He sits in the public gallery and she is escorted to the dock. The charges are read out, and she is asked how she pleads. She pleads guilty. Looking directly at her the judge says, 'I have some great news for you! Someone here, at great personal sacrifice, has paid your debt in full!' He pauses as he watches her lower jaw drop. 'Will you or will you not accept that?'

"She composes herself and then thoughtfully replies, 'It depends, my Lord, on who paid it!' Intuitively she knew that there would be strings attached. She could be exchanging one indebtedness for another.

"The judge looks into the public gallery, gets the nod from the young man, and says, 'Mr Right over there has paid your debt in full. Will you accept that?'

"She becomes choked with emotion as she says, 'Of course I accept, my Lord!' She knows that the strings attached would be a lifetime together in holy wedlock. She marvels at his love for her.

"The judge then asks the prosecution if they object. The prosecution's client has no objection – all he wanted was the money owed. So the judge brings down the hammer and announces, 'I declare you innocent of all charges! You are free to go! Case dismissed!'

"She rushes into the arms of her 'Saviour', and soon they marry to live in covenant with each other for ever – for better, for worse, for richer, for poorer, in sickness and in health."

Pearl seemed mesmerized by this story. I had her full attention. So I continued, "Pearl, you have a debt you owe God that you could never repay. You owe it to Him to love Him with all your heart, soul, and mind every moment of every day you are alive. God is your Judge, and your only honest plea before Him is a plea of guilty!"

She nodded with tears welling up in her eyes. The Holy Spirit was clearly about His wonderful business both convicting and illuminating. How I love the Holy Spirit!

"The most wonderful news you will ever hear is this, Pearl – God, your Judge, says to you, 'My own Son, Jesus Christ, has paid your debt in full'. At the end of His crucifixion He cried with a loud voice, *'Tetelestai'* which means, *'It is finished! It is fully paid! It is completely complete!'* Now He asks you, 'Will you accept that?' The 'strings attached' is a lifetime in covenant with Him – for better, for worse, for richer, for poorer, in sickness and in health. If you say, 'Yes' then God will pronounce you 'innocent of all charges!' This is what 'justification by faith' really means. Justified means 'just-as-if-I'd-never-sinned!' God will give you a brand new start with no more guilt or shame – and no more fear of punishment!"

I looked into Pearl's face. She was overcome with emotion. She looked up at me with a beautiful little smile and said, "I accept! I believe! Yes!"

At that moment I had the unspeakable privilege of witnessing a precious soul re-birthed by God the Holy Spirit. Nevertheless, I told her, "You need to tell the Lord yourself in prayer. I will help you by praying a phrase at a time which you can repeat after me."

"I'd like that," she replied, closing her eyes and bowing her head.

"Lord God, I plead guilty. I have sinned by thought, word and deed – by commission and by omission. I accept that Your Son, Jesus Christ, paid my debt in full when He was crucified. I accept by faith Your forgiveness. I accept Jesus Christ as my personal Saviour. Thank You, thank You, my Father! Lord Jesus, I give my life to You to live together in covenant with You for better, for worse, for richer, for poorer, in sickness and in health. In Jesus' Name, Amen."

I then took out my Gideon's pocket Bible and went through my favourite verses of assurance such as Acts 3:19; Revelation 3:20; John 1:12; and 1 John 5:12, 13. I encouraged her to pray and praise, read the New Testament, attend a Christian fellowship, and wisely share her faith – especially with her husband, Matt. I prayed a closing prayer, we rejoined Matt and Louise for a few minutes, and I left on cloud nine.

There is neither higher privilege nor calling than being an instrument in the Holy Spirit's hands to share the life-changing Gospel of our Lord Jesus Christ.

The next Sunday I baptized Pearl. Her testimony before her baptism was charged with emotion. Matt joined her at the pulpit, placing one arm around her shoulders to help her through. It was beautiful. Although Matt had not yet surrendered himself to the claims of Christ on his life, I asked him to come into the baptism pool with me to help me baptize his wife. The congregation applauded her as Matt and I raised her out of the water, and she delightfully embraced Matt. She was no sooner changed into dry clothing when she pressed me to pray for her to receive the Baptism of the Holy Spirit. This time I gathered not only Ian, Anne, and Clare for prayer, but also their friend, Louise. Matt joined us and this time he stayed as his wife not only received "the Promise of the Father", but also her very own prayer language.

Matt was once again jealous for the supernatural. He was sitting there thinking to himself, "I want this!" but he knew in his heart that giving his life to God was a one-way journey so that he had to take it very seriously.

I realized that Matt was a very clever man, and that he needed some convincing intellectually. He, at the same time had prayed, "Ok, God. If You are listening, I need something more cerebral to help me." Just as he and Pearl were about to leave for home, I came running up to him, and I said, "Matt. I really think you need this book. It's a bit heavier." It was *Mere Christianity* by C.S. Lewis.

He was again amazed at the quick answer to his prayer, and he read it hungrily. I will never forget the Saturday afternoon when he phoned me to ask me to baptize him the next day. Rachel was scheduled to be baptized then. He had already asked her if it would be alright to be baptized after her, and she was thrilled.

"Wait a minute," I replied with a tone I hoped would not dampen his enthusiasm. "I need first of all to be convinced that you have repented of your sin, that you believe that Jesus Christ is your personal Saviour. In other words, do you believe He took your sin and the consequences of your sin when He hung on the cross of Calvary. Have you surrendered your whole life to Him so that you can sincerely call Him Lord?"

"Yes, yes to all those questions. I have finished *Mere Christianity* and having been completely convinced about Jesus Christ and His claim to me; I have given Him my life, my all!"

I cannot explain how overjoyed I was. As I continued talking with him I felt overwhelmed with gratitude to God for His amazing saving grace. I also sensed that He had saved Matt and Pearl not only for heaven, but also for a very fruitful life for Him here on earth.

Pearl very soon began to keep a prayer diary. She would write out her prayers on one page and leave the next page blank so that she could record the answers. She would also paste a star on each prayer that was answered. One day the plumber was around to repair a leak in their bathroom. Pearl was busy writing in her prayer diary when he asked her, "What are you doing?"

"I am writing in my prayer diary," she replied. "Come and see for yourself. These prayers with stars on them are the ones God has already answered and these pages are how He has answered."

This so fascinated the plumber that Pearl was able to witness to him at length and invite him and his wife to church. They came and within two weeks I had the enormous privilege of witnessing them coming to the Saviour!

In all we witnessed about twenty conversions in the three months following that memorable prayer meeting in the back hall.

For the next seven years, Matt and Pearl matured as Christians at a phenomenal rate. Their hunger for God has never abated, and they have faithfully served at the same church where they were saved, giving God all the glory and praise for His work in them.

Chapter 11

The Lord Who Provides
Stories of God's Provision

Clare and I could write so many pages on God's timely provisions for us throughout our time in His service. What we could not afford because our salary was only enough for basics, God made up with amazing provisions. Here are a few more memories that stand out above the rest.

Our First Son

Dr Finley poured over his notes, looked up at Clare, and said, "I have your test results. It does not look good I am afraid. What they indicate is that you are unable to become pregnant. Were you hoping to start a family soon?"

"My husband is at Bible College at present," Clare replied, "And as I am the one working to support him, we had no intention of starting a family until he has completed his studies and settled into paid employment."

"All is not lost, Mrs Henson. We could put you on hormone treatment, but you will need to be on that for a good six months before you intend to become pregnant. I am afraid I could not guarantee that that would work." Then with a sigh he added, "Let's hope for the best!"

Clare was very philosophical when she broke the news to me. She had committed her whole life to Jesus Christ and His cause, even wanting as a young teenager to be a missionary in China, with or without a husband. She had married me because of my single-minded devotion to our

Saviour and Lord. She knew that Jesus Christ was my Great Adventure. She was not and would not be. That really appealed to her. She knew that we would serve the Lord with or without children.

"At least we can do without contraception," I sighed. I knew that Clare would make a brilliant mother, so I must admit that I was somewhat bewildered at the news. Was this all part of God's plan for our lives? That night, after reading the Bible together, we committed this issue into God's hands in prayer.

Some two months later Clare fell ill. She could not hold down any food and sometimes any drink, so she went to the doctor who diagnosed that she must be suffering from gastro-enteritis. She came away with a prescription for antibiotics. When the nausea and vomiting still persisted, Clare returned to see her doctor.

"I think that I could be pregnant," she told him.

"That is impossible, Mrs Henson," he said. "You know that you cannot become pregnant. We could try another antibiotic and anti-nausea medication."

"Please could you give me a pregnancy test, doctor?" Clare politely insisted.

"Alright," he conceded, "But your intuition may be wrong."

Clare's intuition was right! The doctor looked at the test strip in disbelief. "You are pregnant," he announced, "And with your permission I would like to refer you back to your gynaecologist, Dr Finley. This is truly amazing! Congratulations, Mrs Henson!"

Clare threw her arms around me in the car park where I was waiting and, very emotionally announced, "I am pregnant, John. We are going to have a baby! Isn't God good? He is full of surprises! We will have a family after all!"

I could not hide my joy throughout the pregnancy. Nothing, it seemed, could wipe the smile off my face. I was so proud of Clare and so grateful to God. Dr Finley asked Clare whether he could see her through the whole of her pregnancy. "This is a very special case, Mrs Henson," he said, "And your baby is what we consider to be a 'special child'. By that I mean he or she could be your only child. For that reason we will monitor his progress very carefully throughout your pregnancy."

When Clare told me what Dr Finley had said, I said to her, "We must take his statement to be prophetic. Our child will be special! If God grants us any more children, each of them will be special too! Very special!"

Clare worked until she was eight months pregnant. I still had five months to go at Bible College. My request to finish my studies part time back in Bulawayo, so that I could provide for my new family, was turned down. "It will be an opportunity to rely on God completely for His provision," I was told by the principle of the Bible College. Clare and I decided we would not make our need known to any human being. We would trust God who had placed us in this predicament Himself.

We were surprised to find out when Clare resigned from work that she was entitled to maternity pay. That helped a great deal. Then my Bible College principle asked me what rent we were paying and soon after came with an envelope with the amount in cash. An anonymous donor had requested to pay our rent each month. God could be relied on to provide.

Michael's due date was July 7th That day came and went. Dr Finley, after examining Clare and doing an ultra-sound scan on our baby, said, "We will be watching carefully your placental function. I aim to give you a quality baby, so as soon as the placental function drops to a certain point, we will have you in to be induced. That is if he does not come naturally before then."

On July 12 th there was a knock at our front door. There stood Daniel and Cynthia. "We have brought you a few things for your baby," said Cynthia. As we all walked back to their car she explained that she had phoned Bronwyn, a fellow student's wife, to tell her that on account of her rheumatic condition, her doctor had strongly advised her not to have any more children. She had baby kit, and she wondered whether any of the students' pregnant wives needed any things for their babies. Bronwyn had told her that Clare was expecting any day now and that we "had nothing for our baby."

The back seats in their estate car were laid flat, and it was loaded to the roof with baby kit. In there was a large pedigree pram; a brand new push chair; a stack of terri-nappies; a large steri-nappy bucket with a large quantity of steri-nappy powder; baby grows, some still in their plastic wrappers; jumpers and booties; food for us and very helpful aids for Clare. Cynthia had thought of everything. Clare and I stood there with our mouths open.

"You can't do this for us, Cynthia," I said, "This must have cost you a fortune and you hardly know us!"

"I have to!" she replied.

"What do you mean, you have to?" asked Clare.

"We had our two children when Daniel was pastor at our first church," she explained. "The members there believed that Daniel should have secular employment full-time to support his family and fit in the pastoring in the evenings and at weekends. Daniel, on the other hand, believed what the Bible says about preachers living off the Gospel. Our wage from the church was so low that we had to do without so much. At times I would have to water down the milk we gave our children. I ended up so bitter that we left that church. Now we are doing much better, and I have forgiven those church members. However," she paused to wipe away tears from her eyes, "I feel that to be healed of the hurt, I need to do for someone else what I would have loved to have been done for us." She then waved her hand towards the contents of her car and said, "and here it all is!"

We were now all in tears. Clare took the initiative to give Cynthia a big hug. Daniel and I then embraced. It was a very holy moment. A huge burden appeared to lift off both of them and soon their tears turned to laughter. So did ours. Michael was born at 4.55pm on July 18th. Had Michael not been delivered naturally by 5pm, Dr Finley would have performed a caesarean section on Clare. His "prophecies" about Michael being both "special" and "quality" have come true.

Our First Holiday

In mid-September we packed up all our belongings to return to Zimbabwe. My little family was then given a two-week holiday before I began to pastor a little church in Redcliff and the neighbouring town of Kwe Kwe, beginning on October 1st, 1980.

We were much better off than Daniel and Cynthia had been at their first church. I was expected to be full-time pastor, our rent was paid by the church, and we managed on my salary. In April, 1981, we booked our first four week holiday at a self-catering cottage on the South Coast in South Africa. We were exhausted and badly needed the break. The only problem was that we only had enough savings to pay for petrol to get there.

We were to leave on the Tuesday, so I said to Clare on the Sunday morning before church, "Sweetheart, we need God to supply the money for our holiday today. Tomorrow we will need to buy our traveller's cheques. This is cutting it a bit fine, I know."

We had a box on a small table at the entrance to the church into which our members placed their tithes and offerings. Our treasurer and another church member would count it up after the service had ended. As he was about to climb into his car to drive home, I asked, "Has anything special come in to the box this morning?"

He looked a little bewildered at me, shrugged his shoulders and said, "No, nothing special. Were you expecting anything?"

"Not really," I said, knowing that I had hoped there was an envelope in there that had my name on it and a post-script, "for your holiday" written on it.

Our Sunday dinner was disturbed by a phone call from Daniel. He asked whether he and his dear wife Nettie could come for a cup of tea that afternoon. "Sure!" I had replied, "We would love to see you!" Normally we were the ones visiting them. They adored Michael and were like surrogate grandparents to him. Whenever we visited them, we would come away with packets of groceries and home cooked cakes and biscuits.

They wanted to know all about our holiday plans and were delighted that we were having a "well earned break". As they were about to leave, Daniel leaned out of the window of his car and said, "By the way, Pastor John, I have left an envelope on the mantelpiece in your living room. It has a few dollars in it. Please buy Michael a few toys with it. God bless you all. Have a wonderful holiday!" and he sped away.

The envelope contained enough money in it to sponsor our whole holiday and enable us to buy some things to bring home. I climbed in the car and rushed around to their home to thank them from the bottom of my heart for being God's means to answer our prayer. "Oh it's nothing," he said, "I have no need for the money. You all just go and enjoy a great holiday. You deserve it!"

Our Mercedes Benz

Years later we booked again for a holiday in a self-catering cottage on the South Coast of Natal Province in South Africa. We had recently acquired a very old Mercedes 200D and were excited about our first long trip in it. However, when we arrived at the Zimbabwe border with South Africa I became very anxious about unusual noises from the engine. When we started out again for the long journey to my mother's home in Boksburg I voiced my concerns about the noises to Clare.

"These noises make me very uneasy about taking this car on from my mom's home to the coast. I think we will need to pray that she will lend us her car or else that God would provide in some other way," I said anxiously.

By the time we arrived in Boksburg we were very grateful that the car had kept going, despite the noise. We greeted my mother and step-father and went into their house for a good cup of tea. I did not mention our car worries. We were scheduled to stay there for two nights so there was plenty of time to talk about our need. I also thought I might find a garage to repair the fault the next day.

However that night my brother David phoned my mother from Gutu in Zimbabwe and asked to speak to me. "John," he began, "I have 4,200 Rand in South Africa in Mom's account. Please could I trouble you to try and find a Mercedes 240D for me whilst you are on holiday down there?"

"I would love to do that for you, David," I replied. "I'll phone my friend John who owns a second hand car business in Johannesburg and see if he can help."

I phoned John and, after catching up with his news, asked him to help me find a Mercedes 240D in good condition for my brother. "One has just come onto the forecourt," he replied. "I have not yet checked it over but the asking price is 4,200 Rand."

"I'll take it, John!" I said excitedly.

"I cannot guarantee its condition," he replied. "As I said, it has only just come in, and I have not yet checked it over!"

"My brother wants me to spend 4,200 Rand, the exact asking price. I see this as an answer to prayer. We leave for the South Coast on Thursday, and I would like to collect it tomorrow morning!"

As soon as I returned to my mother's home with this beautiful lime-green Mercedes, I phoned my brother. I was genuinely excited for him! He was thrilled too, and after I had given him a full description he said, "John, I will need to do the paper-work to import it into Zimbabwe. That will take some time, and anyway I cannot collect it for another month. How about you use it on your holiday? That way you can check out any faults and have them repaired before I come to collect it!"

I came off the phone marvelling at God's provision. We had a fabulous journey in that car, and there were no faults to sort out by the time we returned it to my mother's house. I was very anxious as soon as I started up our own Mercedes. We prayed earnestly that it would at least get us home. Our money was spent so we could not have it seen to in South Africa.

We were 100 miles into Zimbabwe on the very lonely road from Beit Bridge to Masvingo when there was an almighty noise from the engine. I took the car out of gear and coasted into a lay-by which just happened to be there. I lifted the bonnet to look vaguely at the engine when a man in a large BMW pulled in to the lay-by to ask if we needed any help. I asked him to take Clare and our three sons into the Mercedes garage in Masvingo and they sped off. Two and a half hours later a tow-truck arrived to tow me into Masvingo some 80 miles away.

The mechanic took the cam cover off the engine to find that all the cam-riders had broken. The pump that assisted the brakes had disintegrated, and a part had lodged onto the timing gear, and the timing chain had snapped the cam riders. He said that it would take at least two weeks to order up the parts. I was about to ask if I could use the telephone to phone my brother to come and fetch us when I noticed my brother's father-in-law's car in the service bay.

"Is that Mr Jackson's car?" I asked the receptionist.

"Yes! I am about to phone him to tell him that it is ready for collection."

"Could you ask him whether we could deliver it to him?" I asked, "His farm borders on my brother's and if we can get that far tonight, my brother could run us up to Harare tomorrow."

Mr Jackson, on hearing about our predicament, immediately offered to lend us his car until ours was repaired. A few months later my brother came in to some more money in South Africa, and this time he clubbed together with my mother to buy us our own Mercedes 240D. He told me that my attitude towards him getting one had convinced him to do all he could to get me one too.

Comforting My Mother

One Thursday I received a cheque for $900. I thanked God for it and banked it, certain that God would show me what it was to be spent on. The next day Clare and I were going into the centre of Harare. Before we set out I felt a compulsion to pick up our passports and take them too. On the way in I said to Clare, "I feel that we need to apply for visas for South Africa."

"What do you want to do that for?" she asked. "Our next holiday is due in six months time. It only takes a week to get visas!"

"I just feel led to. I don't know why," I replied.

The lady at the South African Trade Mission told me to return the next Friday when our visas would be processed.

The following Tuesday my mother phoned in an emotional state. "Please pray for Bill," she pleaded. "He is having real difficulty breathing, and he has been rushed to hospital. Son, I am very worried about him!"

When I put down the phone I said to Clare, "I now know why God supplied that $900 last Thursday and I now know why I was led to apply for visas for South Africa. Bill has been rushed to hospital with breathing difficulties, and I believe he is not going to make it! God wants us there for mom!"

Three days later my sister Nora Jean phoned. "I have really bad news for you, John!" She went silent with emotion, and I instantly knew what was to come. "Bill passed away at 10.30 this morning."

"I am so very sorry, Nora Jean," I began. "You were there when dad died, and now you are there when Bill died. I thank you from the bottom of my heart!" When my father died some seven years before, it was during the Rhodesian war, and I was on military duty. "I would like to speak to mom," I concluded.

"John, she is in a worse condition than when dad died! I do not think she is in any state to speak to anyone."

"I have news for her that will comfort her, so please let me speak to her," I insisted.

Moments later I heard my mother's softened, shaky voice. "Is that you my son?"

"Yes it's me, mom, and I have news for you. Clare, David and I will be on the next airplane to you!"

She instantly composed herself so that with a stronger voice she said, "But son, you will need to apply for visas and that takes some time."

"I applied last Friday and was told that they would be ready for me today!" I said.

"But son, how can you afford to fly? I know you are always on a tight budget!"

"Last Thursday I received a cheque for $900, and I am sure that that will cover the airfares. I will go in right away and I will let you know as soon as we have the tickets." I was then overcome with emotion, not only because of my empathy with my mother at the untimely loss of her second husband, but also at the foreknowledge and comfort of our wonderful Saviour and Lord. He is so fittingly described as *the God of all comfort,* and as *the Man of sorrows, acquainted with grief.*

Our tickets came to $906. We were with my mother the next morning. We were there when she met with Bill's family, and we were by her side through the funeral.

A Home of our Own

We moved into the church manse at Belvedere in June 1983. It was a very comfortable four-bedroom house, but it stood in the back yard of the church building. That fact often cost us our privacy. On several occasions a church member would wander into our kitchen to raid our fridge for milk because there was not enough at the church kitchen. The beggars in Harare would pester us too, believing that we would be a soft touch. After five years of this we implored the Lord for a home of our own. My salary at that time was $7,000 a year and so the most a mortgage company would lend us was $21,000. That amount would scarcely enable us to buy a studio flat, let alone a three-bedroom house. If God were to answer our prayers, He would need to perform a miracle.

Val, a senior member in our church, phoned me at 4pm on that Sunday afternoon. "We need you to come here immediately!" she said with an urgent tone.

"What's the matter, Val, why the urgency?" I asked.

"Please don't ask questions, John – just come!" she said impatiently.

I replaced the phone and stared blankly at Clare. "What's that all about?" she asked.

"I don't know, my darling. Val asked if we could go there immediately. Something dreadful must have happened."

We rushed to 29 Dublin Road to find a VW Golf parked in the driveway. We parked our car and rushed to the front door. Brian, Ian and Val's son answered the door. "Thanks for coming so quickly," he said, ushering us into the living room.

Val broke free from Ian's embrace and came over to embrace us, followed by Ian. Together they explained what had happened. Their daughter Sue had been one of the very few women to pass the very rigorous selection course into the Rhodesian SAS during our eight-year war. When the new Zimbabwe Government in April 1980 disbanded the SAS, Sue had emigrated to South Africa. There she had been recruited by the South African Intelligence Service to spy for them against the African National Congress who had a base in Harare. She travelled to Zimbabwe often, sometimes under cover as a make-up artist for a film company; sometimes to spend time with her parents.

Sue had liaised with a group of four Zimbabwe operatives, usually meeting them outside her father's shop. They had been captured by the notorious Zimbabwe CIO (Central Intelligence Office) and had promised to divulge their secrets within forty-eight hours of their capture. The South African Intelligence Service had contacted Brian to instruct him that he had until 5pm on that Monday to get his parents out of Zimbabwe. So Brian raced up from Cape Town to Harare. Val had phoned me immediately after he had explained the situation to them. Val had said very little on the phone in case the CIO were already on to them and were listening to her calls.

Ian and Val had planned to retire to Cape Town and were expecting an estate agent to come at 10am the next morning to put their house on the market. They had taken their Nissan car to a body shop for a complete re-spray in preparation for their emigration to South Africa. Now they were in turmoil. Their old Mercedes needed new tyres and a tow bar so that they could take it and their trailer, laden with their most precious possessions, on the very long journey south. Amazingly our Mercedes was the same model and age as theirs, we had just put new tyres all round, and we had a tow bar. So whilst Clare helped Ian and Val choose and pack their most precious belongings, Brian and I swapped our car wheels for theirs and relocated our tow hitch to their car.

Clare and I were emotionally and physically exhausted when we retired home that night. We were back at 29 Dublin Road the next morning to pack the final things into their car and trailer. Just as Ian was about to climb into his car, he remembered his appointment with the estate agent at 10am. So he rushed back indoors to phone and cancel the appointment.

Ian and Val, in convoy with Brian in his VW Golf, left Harare for the last time at about 9am. They crossed the Zimbabwe-South Africa border at 3pm, and the CIO was around at 29 Dublin Road at about 5.30pm. Abraham, who worked as Ian and Val's domestic and gardener, informed them that Clare and I were sure to know where they had gone since I was their church minister. At about 5.45pm four burly men climbed out of their car at the church manse to confront Clare about Ian and Val's whereabouts. Had I been there I am sure they would have taken me away for questioning. Clare told them that all she knew was that they had left for South Africa in a hurry to attend to some family crisis there.

Over their radio they verified that Ian and Val had crossed the border at 3pm, and then they climbed back into their car and left.

Over the next few months we would have black "newcomers" attend our multiracial Sunday morning service. We were fairly sure they worked for the CIO. We were also fairly sure that our telephone was tapped for a while.

A couple of weeks after Ian and Val's departure we received a letter from them via their solicitor in Harare. They were afraid that the CIO might seize any letter addressed to us that was postmarked from South Africa. To protect us they were going to send letters via their solicitor. In this letter they asked us to pack up their home and arrange with their bank for their emigration from Zimbabwe, citing ill health as the reason for them not returning to Zimbabwe to do it themselves. With the letter came a Power of Attorney. "Finally," they wrote, "We strongly believe that God wants us to sell you our home at 29 Dublin Road for what you can afford. We do not believe you should live any longer on top of the church in Belvedere. We currently owe our mortgage company around $18,000. We will accept anything above that."

I read that "finally paragraph" twice before reading it a third time to Clare. This was the miracle we had prayed for! A beautiful three bedroom home set on almost an acre of magnificent garden in a sought-after suburb of Harare and just a couple of hundred yards from a truly great Christian primary school. God was doing exceedingly abundantly above all that we had asked for.

I did write to say that all we could raise was $25,000; that their home was worth at least $110,000 and I therefore offered to sell it for them and somehow, legally, get the money down to them in South Africa. They fired back a rebuttal stating that God had told them to sell us their home for what we could afford and that they accepted $25,000 willingly. "What you have done for us throughout our time in your church, and what you had risked for us in our escape, were incalculable. We are absolutely delighted that the home that we have so loved would be owned and occupied by you!" they concluded.

We managed, with the Power of Attorney, to emigrate for Ian and Val, as well as ship all their furniture and money down to them. I drove their gleaming re-sprayed Nissan all the way down to Cape Town and brought their old Mercedes all the way back to sell in Zimbabwe for them. On my return journey I spent the night with Clare's sister, Cathy and brother-in-law, Robert. He asked me all about how to become a Christian, and although I was thrilled to do that, I was not able to "clinch the deal". He wanted time to think about all I had told him. Within a month he went into the Pretoria Military Hospital to have surgery on his gums. He was given a general anaesthetic and within minutes he was dead. I could only hope he had given his heart to Christ before that tragic event. I believe that God could have arranged for Ian and Val's Nissan to be in for a re-spray at the time of their escape so that I would later need to do that journey to speak to Robert's heart about eternal issues.

Our Up and Away Day

Talk about God arranging things here on earth, we were four years into our ownership of 29 Dublin Road when in March, 1991, I prayed to God, "Gracious Father, this April will mark the twenty-first year that I have been your child. This year is Clare's twenty-first too. Should You want to give us a twenty first birthday present, what we would really like is a trip over to the UK, because that is where our grandparents came from."

Clare's father's parents came from Edinburgh in Scotland, and her mother's parents came from Forfar, a small town north of Edinburgh. My father's parents came from the West Midlands and Wales, and my great grandfather was also the Reverend John Henson. We had never travelled to the UK before and we certainly did not have the wherewithal to travel then.

To my astonishment the very next week British Airways sponsored full page adverts in the national newspapers for their forthcoming "Up and Away Day" to "get the world flying after the Gulf War". All we had to do was apply and write a slogan. God gave us the faith to believe that this was going to be our twenty-first birthday present, and we applied. British Airways staff then took the thousands of applications up in a hot-air balloon where they randomly picked out the required number of winners.

"Congratulations, Rev Henson," the lady on the telephone said to me, "I am phoning on behalf of British Airways. You and your wife have won free tickets for our 'Up and Away Day'. You will fly on April 23rd, leaving Harare Airport at 2100 hours. Your return flight will also be free but you need to let us know as soon as possible when you would like to return so that we can confirm your booking in writing and issue your tickets."

I could not wait to tell Clare so I ran down the road to Gateway Primary School where she taught, found her classroom and knocked on the door. Clare stopped what she was doing to walk across her classroom to open the door. As soon as she opened the door, my pent-up emotion poured out. I just stood there crying, unable to say a word.

Clare closed the classroom door behind her and, throwing her arms around me, gently asked, "What has happened, John?"

"We have won those tickets to the UK!" I blurted out. "God has given us the twenty-first birthday present we asked Him for! We are off to the UK on the twenty-third of this month. Praise the Lord, my sweetheart!"

"That's a relief to hear that," she replied. "I thought that with that amount of emotion there must have been a death in the family or some other tragedy." Then pulling away from me a bit she looked me in the eye and said, "God is just so good to us, and I do praise Him! Do we have it in writing?"

"No, not yet. They phoned to give me the news and as soon as we give them a return date they will confirm it in writing."

We arrived at Harare Airport to find the British Airways staff all dressed in period costume. The lady at the check-in desk looked at my ticket and passport and said, "So you are a Reverend! I think we can put you and your wife in business class! Enjoy your flight!"

Tim, an elder from the Gospel Centre in North London, met us at London Heathrow. He had organised for me to preach in a different church each of the four Sundays of our "holiday". His father had bought us an old Vauxhall car and with it we travelled three thousand five hundred miles around England and Scotland. The gratuities we received at the churches we preached at paid all our expenses throughout our stay in the UK. We did spend nights with family and church members along the way, but we also had precious times together at various bed and breakfast places too. The money we took in traveller's cheques from Zimbabwe we spent on presents for ours sons and the relatives who cared for them whilst we were away. We also bought a keyboard for the church back home.

Christian Life Centre, Horsham

It was whilst we were travelling around the UK we sensed God's call to us to come over and pastor a church here. The following September we received a formal request from Tim to pastor the Horsham Pentecostal Church. The pastor had left some six months previous and recently one of the elders had also left. Tim feared that the church was collapsing, and the executive council agreed that we would be the right people, under God, to put it back together again. God wonderfully provided the finance to fly the family over here and we began to pastor the church on December 1st 1992. We quickly renamed the church Christian Life Centre, since we were far keener to have new converts than members of other churches who may know what "Pentecostal" meant.

The church building was in a very shoddy condition. The back hall was particularly run down. It had kitchen units one end that were sinking on the rotting floorboards. The toilets were revolting. There was a small room coming off the back hall that was very dilapidated and full of junk. "We must renovate the toilets and back hall as a priority," I told the church. "I am embarrassed to walk back there."

"We do not have the money," said our treasurer. "It would be foolish to go ahead without the wherewithal." Others agreed.

"I have been involved in the building of two large churches in high density suburbs in Harare," I said. "We did not have the money up front, but we went ahead anyway. God honoured our faith and provided as we went along. I believe He wants us to renovate this whole church, and we must begin with the simplest and least costly – the back hall and toilets. He will provide as we go along. We could arrange for work parties with volunteers, and you'll be surprised at how much we can achieve for free."

We had plans drawn up for the back hall and for the main hall. We wanted to put in a mezzanine floor in both. In that way we could double the usable space of the building. We also wanted to do away with the wooden flooring and dark wooden panelling around the walls. The frosted glass windows we wanted exchanged for UPVC double-glazed clear windows. We would be fitting a completely new central heating system to replace the expensive and ineffective electric heaters. The lighting would be bright. The front double wooden doors we would replace with double-glazed see-through doors. At the entrance we wanted a reception area and a soundproof mother-and-child room. Over the back hall we wanted a big church office and over the main hall we wanted one long room and three smaller rooms for Sunday school and youth activities.

By now Clare and I had returned to Zimbabwe where we had sold 29 Dublin Road, emigrated and shipped some of our furniture back to Horsham. With the equity from our house sale we offered to buy the manse. That would have enabled the church to accomplish much of the proposed building work. Despite much persuasive talk my offer was turned down by the central trustees of the denomination. Their policy was to have manses "just in case there is a change of pastor in the future."

Clare and I could not afford, on my wage, to buy our own home, even with our equity as a deposit. So we opted to sink our money into the renovations at the church. From past experience, we were confident that God would more than make up for it as He is "no man's debtor."

A work party was formed of male volunteers from the church and on one Saturday we managed to rip up all the rotting floorboards in the back hall; destroy the derelict old kitchen; crush up the bricks to form hardcore for a new floor; and lay sand and plastic sheeting ready for the concrete. The concrete floor was poured the next week. Over the next couple of months, we built a lovely new kitchen, revamped the toilets, put in a new floor with the staircase up to it, and completed a great office upstairs. As we proceeded we were given additional finance from various sources, and we were thrilled with the finished product. Over the years that followed our contribution to the project was repaid to us.

Then we were prepared to launch out on the main project – that of completely modernizing the main hall. When we began to rip up the old floorboards and demolish the middle rooms and balcony above them, we had £8000 in the bank, which included a grant from our Church Headquarters of £5000. That first Sunday after operations began we all joined a charismatic Baptist Church for a combined church service. By the second Sunday we had part of the new floor in place so we reconvened our Sunday service there. To support the giant joists for the mezzanine floor we had to dig metre-cubed holes near the existing walls onto which steel pillars were secured. It was a massive job. And it swallowed up the money in the bank!

All the floorboards and the wooden panelling from the walls of the main hall we placed outside the main entrance of the church with a for-sale sign next to them. An antique dealer from across the road saw the wood and offered to pay for all the electrics, all the lighting, and all the decoration, including paint brushes and rollers, in exchange for the wood. "Americans just love old English pine, and I'll sell it all on to them," he confidently assured us.

One of our new members approached me to tell me that although he now worked for a computer installation company, he was a fully qualified electrician, and he wanted to install all the electrics for free. He did a brilliant job!

I remember one Sunday, Alex, our project manager, asking whether we had any money in the building fund. "I think there is about £200," I had said.

"Pity that," said Alex, "The Builder's Centre have told me that if we do not pay for the materials we have had from them by this Friday they will close our account. We owe them £4000."

I went across to Ian and Anne who were counting the money from the Tithes and Offerings box. "Look at this," said Ian, waving two cheques, "£4020 has come in to the building fund today!"

I called Alex over to show him what Ian had just written into the record book. "Here is the money you said we need! Praise the Lord!"

Several weeks later when we had in place all the wooden frames for the partitions at the front entrance and mother-and-child room, I approached Alex for another progress report. "When is the double glazing coming for those frames?" I asked.

"I know that we are very low on funds again, John, so I am not pushing the supplier. It will cost £4950 and they expect a cheque on completion. They will fit all that glass in one day." Alex was right, we were very low on funds. We were down to our last £100!

On a Tuesday morning at 9:45am the glazing company's white van pulled up outside the church front door. The workmen very quickly opened the double doors of the van and began carrying the large glass units up into the church. The driver apologized for not coming the previous Friday. Their van had broken down and needed repairs. It was returned to them the night before. When he reminded me that they required a cheque by the end of the day, I broke out in a sweat. I thought of raiding my two credit cards as much as I hated doing that. I was just about to leave the scene to go up to my office where I intended to fall on my knees in prayer when I heard a voice behind me.

"John!" It was Charles, a middle aged man that I had had the privilege of bringing to faith in the Lord Jesus some months before. He had felt that our church worship was a bit rowdy for him and had found a wonderful evangelical Church of England to be his ideal spiritual home. "As you know I often pass this way into town, and I have been fascinated to see the progress on your building project," he said as we moved away from the activity at the front door. "Could I have a private word with you?"

I took him up to my office. It was now 10am. Charles rather sheepishly explained to me that he had felt it laid on his heart to offer a grant to us to help us in our endeavour. I tell it that way because Charles was upper-class. He spoke that way. He had been schooled at the famous Eton College.

"That would be very much appreciated," I said. "We could have a written agreement if you like. How much would you like to grant us?"

"£5000," he replied.

I nearly fell off my chair! "Incredible!" I exclaimed. "The glaziers that you saw in the church want a cheque for £4950 for their work today. Not only is the amount you are offering perfect, so is your timing. They told me that they were meant to have come on Friday, but their van broke down. They only got it back from repairs yesterday evening. Your grant is an amazing answer to prayer. Well done for hearing the Lord and then obeying Him as you have now done!"

Now it was Charles' turn to get excited and emotional. "John! It came to me on Friday that I should offer you this grant!" He had the cheque out of his shirt pocket and was waving it in his right hand. He shook his head before saying, "I want to give you this money, John. I do not need it myself. I do not want you to pay any of it back. It means the world to me that I have become the answer to your prayers! Praise be to the Lord!"

The project did keep me on my knees. I was determined to trust God for His provision without having to canvass any donations from man. I also rolled up my sleeves to spend at least three days a week working hard on the project. I sometimes raided my credit cards to be paid back in time. Others in the church, both men and women, volunteered to help too. Just before Clare and I left Horsham for Livingston, Scotland, we managed to complete the whole project with the construction of a toilet for the disabled. I can only guess that we managed, by God's glorious and timely provisions, to complete the estimated £250,000 renovations for about half that price.

Reunion in New Zealand

In June, 2003, I wrote an email to my brother David and his wife, Annalie. They had been ordered by the Zimbabwe Government to vacate their farm near Gutu. I knew that the whole experience had given them huge stress and heartbreak. I sought to comfort them somehow before they left for their new life in New Zealand at the end of the week. As I concluded the email, I felt a strong desire to see them again soon, so I added a postscript, "We are really going to pray that God would enable us to spend Christmas with you this year in New Zealand."

That very night we received a phone call from Callun, a church member. "Could I call around to see you and Clare?" he asked.

"We are in so you are most welcome," I replied.

Over a cup of tea he said, "Sue and I have been talking about your brother having to leave his farm in Zimbabwe and emigrate to New Zealand. We feel led to pay for air tickets for you to spend Christmas with them this year."

I nearly fell off my chair! "I wrote only this morning to my brother. I felt led to tell him that Clare and I would be praying that we would be able to spend Christmas with them. Now I can write back to him to tell him that God has already answered that prayer. Praise the Lord for His goodness. Thank you, Callun, thank you very much!!"

Callun and Sue paid for Clare, Dave (our youngest son) and me to spend the holiday of a lifetime on both North and South Island, New Zealand.

Oasis Christian Centre, Livingston

Towards the end of 2006 Clare had an operation on her sinuses. When she was recovering she felt compelled to sort out the large number of family and holiday photographs we had in a large box in the lounge. When that was completed she began to spring clean and redecorate the manse. The children had left home, and so she also tackled the clearing out of the loft space. As she was doing all this she heard God's still small voice telling her, "You are not doing this for yourself, but for others!" It was so clear that she wrote it down in her journal and shared it with her supervisor.

At the same time she had a sense that God was about to do really great things for us. This excited and energised her. Then she read the Gospel story of the Lord Jesus borrowing Peter's boat from which to preach to the multitudes. In her mind's eye she saw her name written on the bow of a boat, and she heard the Lord ask her, "Can I use your boat?"

"Yes, Lord! You are most welcome to use my boat!" she replied.

"Will you take it out into the deep?" He asked.

"I have done that before, my Lord, and it was hard. Nevertheless if that is what You want of me, I'll do it again," she replied.

In the November of 2006 we felt led to put our little one-bed roomed flat up for sale. We were not sure what we would do with the equity but were praying for our own home and hoped that our new local trustees would be able to sell us the manse.

In the January of 2007 we were invited to have prophetic ministry in a church in Yapton, West Sussex. The small group of "prophets" knew nothing about us except our names which were stuck to our jumpers. We had several words but the one that really spoke to me was about my need for new direction and new vision. I was told that this direction would come to me in a clearer way than I had experienced before.

Shortly after that we, as a church, held an "Extreme Dream Day." We were encouraged to bring all kinds of magazines, a large card, glue, and scissors. Then we were instructed to go through the magazines and to cut out any words or pictures that immediately appealed to us. We had to paste these onto the card to form a "dream-board". Later, Clare and I did the same exercise as a couple. On this dream-board Clare pasted a large picture of a pier going out into a lake with snow-capped mountains in the background. What appealed to her was the way the pier encouraged her out into the deep – reminding her of the Lord's request to her to take her boat out into the deep. Next to the pier picture she pasted a ballerina because she loved ballet. On the snow-capped mountain beyond the pier I had pasted the words, "The Promised Land".

At the end of that month I received a "Leader-to-Leader" email giving a list of churches badly in need of a pastor. Out of curiosity I read through the list, and the church in Livingston gripped my heart. I looked it up on the internet to find out where it was. Finding that it was in Scotland, I began to reminisce about the wonderful family holidays we had enjoyed in Scotland. I also wondered if the famous missionary/explorer David Livingstone came from there. I then tried to put Livingston out of my mind. It went to the back of my mind but every now and then would come back to the front. I had been led by God this way before so I asked the Lord that if He wanted us to make a move there, He confirm it in no uncertain way to Clare – without my involvement.

In February 2007 we at last completed on the sale of our flat and formally applied to buy the manse.

In March, Clare and I went out to Southern Africa where both of us spoke at a large conference in Pretoria. Clare wondered if this is what the Lord Jesus meant in calling her out into the deep. When we returned we held a church-away weekend at which one of our speakers challenged us to be prepared to "move out of our comfort zones" and become involved in church planting. I told Clare, much to her astonishment and discomfort, that God may be speaking to us about moving, and that we must be open to that.

In May I went to a special Minister-in-Training day in St Albans. One of the speakers had been a pastor at the Livingston Elim Church, and he told us of some of his experiences there. This obviously re-ignited the thoughts of Livingston needing a pastor. Was the vacancy still there after all these months? After the meetings we were placed in small groups for prayer and prophecy. In my group was a worship leader called Joel, and God gave me a word through him.

"I have a very strong word for you, John," he began. "It's the word 'legacy'! I believe that the Lord is telling you that you are going to be leaving a legacy. It will be a legacy of your faithful service to Him."

"That is a good word to me," I responded. "I am writing a book entitled *Privileged Witness - Stories of a Local Pastor*, and that will be a legacy, at least for my family."

"Actually," interjected a pastor well known to me, "I have had a vision of you going up into your loft and bringing down from there old suitcases – suitcases you thought you might never use again. I believe that this word is linked with Joel's about a legacy. I believe you will be leaving Horsham."

I was stunned. Just two weeks before, our youngest son, David had returned home from university. He had completed his degree and had brought all his belongings home in old suitcases. After emptying them, Clare had taken them around to the side of the house to be binned. When I found them there, I had felt compelled to rescue them and quietly put them up in the loft "just in case!" Clare caught me doing so and asked me, "What are you doing with those old suitcases?"

"I am taking them up to the loft – who knows, they may come in handy sometime," I said.

"John, I have recently tidied out the loft! We will never use those suitcases again!"

"I know! But I still feel that I should take them there!" I now felt very awkward carrying them up the ladder and placing them neatly in the very tidy loft.

When I returned from St Albans, I related the prophecies to Clare. This was the first time she knew that I had had a leading about Livingston. Now that leading was being confirmed, and I knew I had to do something about it. Clare was very distressed by the news, and although she knew I must follow it up, she hoped and prayed that someone else had heeded the call there.

I phoned the regional superintendent for Scotland. He confirmed that Livingston was still without a pastor. He took some details from me and phoned my regional superintendent for a reference. Soon after I was put in contact with the one remaining elder at Livingston, and an interview date was set. It was to be on the Friday afternoon, and I requested that I also preach on the Sunday. I wanted to know God's hand on me in the pulpit and with the members.

The interview seemed to go well, but Clare was going through turmoil. It was very distressing for me to watch. I desperately wanted God Himself to confirm in no uncertain way to her heart that this is what He was talking about when He had asked her to go out into the deep. Her counselling ministry was being so blessed by God in Horsham, she was so settled there, and she recalled vividly the traumatic time she went through when we first came to the United Kingdom.

When we entered Oasis Christian Centre that Sunday, we looked up to the screen that displayed the songs that were to be sung, and the background was a long pier, lit up on both sides and with open gates at the end of it. Clare was stunned! She had all the confirmation she needed! She remembered a word from a dear lady in the Horsham Church about God opening doors for us which no man could shut. The gates were open! I recognised that I had seen that scene before. However at that time I did not remember the dream board Clare and I had done together. Clare said nothing about it to me then either!

We returned home and at the beginning of the week Clare was telling the Lord that it was just too difficult for her. She was asking God to give her the grace to face and cope with the trauma of leaving Horsham and launching out into the unknown. Just then she noticed in her New Testament reading a cross-reference to Deuteronomy 30 where God tells Moses, *"The commandment that I give you this day is not too difficult for you, nor is it far off. The word is very near you, in your mouth and in your heart, that you may do it."* As she read on into the next chapter she read about Moses handing the responsibilities of the leadership of Israel over to Joshua. She was now more than convinced, yet she still did not tell me. She was waiting for the phone call from Livingston. A part of her still wanted them to say no to us.

That Friday I was comforting a missionary friend of mine who had just received the tragic news from his son in South Africa that his wife had suddenly died from a heart attack. The phone rang, and the regional superintendent of Scotland was on the line. "Oasis Christian Centre in Livingston would like to call you as their new pastor. If you want time to think and pray about it, that's fine."

"We accept!" I said. "I will break the news to Clare now, and I am sure she'll agree."

"That is a real answer to prayer," he said. "When do you think you will be able to start?"

"God warned me not to go out of here in haste. Clare and I are so involved in so many things here in Horsham, and it will take time and care to relinquish them. We want to finish strong. We would also want to buy our own home there, so when we move will also depend on when we can complete on the purchase. I shall keep you posted."

"Great! Welcome to Scotland – 'the Promised Land'!"

I phoned Clare who was in prayer with two Anglican friends. She had shared everything with them and they had told her that God's leading was absolutely clear. "Sweetheart, I have just received the call from Scotland. They want us!"

"Is that it then?" she asked.

"That's it, my darling!" I replied.

When I sat down again with my friend, I asked him where he would have gone if he had not had to return so quickly to South Africa. He said he would first have gone to Livingston near Edinburgh to stay with an old friend! I told him our story, and he became so excited for us. This gave me such a settled peace for which I am very thankful.

When I returned home, Clare poured out her whole story. God had indeed answered my prayer for her! That night Clare and I watched on TV the principle ballerina for the Royal Ballet dancing her last dance in that role. We both remembered the ballerina she had pasted next to the picture of the pier on our dream board!

During the next week we told our story to each member of our leadership team separately. Our Sunday school superintendent exclaimed, "I thought that the children were to leave home, not the parents!"

That Sunday we told our story and announced our move to a stunned congregation. For so many of them we had played a big part in their salvation, restoration, healing and spiritual growth. The next week we were telling our story to the ministers in the fraternal I had chaired, to the Oasis Crisis Pregnancy Centre members that Clare in particular had served, to the Detention Centre where I had evangelised for the previous ten years, and to the various boards of trustees we had been on. That weekend I was up at Livingston looking for a house and telling the congregation in Oasis Christian Centre our story.

Clare had trusted the Lord to lead me to find a home for us. She had urgent appointments which prevented her from coming too. I found our home – the seller had redecorated throughout, installing a brand new kitchen and bathroom. Although my offer was accepted, when we worked out our finances, we needed another £25,000 for the deposit. This was going to be another test of our faith. At my last men's breakfast I was asked if I needed any special prayer and before I could catch myself I said that I needed another £20,000 towards my deposit. The men prayed for me. Just before I needed that amount in my bank account ready for completion of purchase, one of our church members gave us a cheque for £15,000, a cheque came from another member for £5,000, and someone from oversees sent us the final £5,000.

We completed our purchase on September 7, 2007, and we arrived here in Livingston to be handed our keys on September 11, which was our thirty-first wedding anniversary. On Clare's dream board were a number of pictures to do with house and garden. Since leaving 29 Dublin Road for Jesus Christ and His cause, it has been her dream (and mine) to have a home of our own. And God brought it about – on our anniversary!

A Study on How to Share Our Faith

The Message of Evangelism

By far the greatest privilege and joy this side of heaven is to be used by the Holy Spirit to bring someone else into a personal and meaningful relationship with the Lord Jesus Christ. "*...there is joy in the presence of the angels of God over one sinner who repents,*" (Luke 15:10). Remember that Hebrews 12:2 tells us to "*Look unto Jesus...who for the joy that was set before Him endured the cross, despising the shame....*" **Every person who is saved by His grace becomes *a reward for His sacrifice*.** In fact, the Lord Jesus Himself said "*...there is more joy in heaven over one sinner who repents than over ninety-nine just persons who need no repentance.*" (Luke 15:7). Likewise the Father's heart overflows with pure joy when the prodigal returns – see Luke 15:32.

As we draw near to God (Father, Son and Holy Spirit) we discover there is a cry from His heart for lost humanity. He has a passion for souls! Calvary's cross is infallible proof of that! The more profoundly touched we are by Calvary love, the more passion we have to share that love. Having filled us, it flows as a river from us. This passion for the lost is more easily caught than taught. The woman at the well in John 4 caught a passion for the lost from the Master Evangelist and "*...then left her waterpot, went her way into the city, and said to the men, 'Come, see a man who told me all things that I ever did. Could this be the Christ?'*" (John 4:28,29).

There are five great truths that must be emphasized in all evangelistic work. They must be soaked in specific and earnest prayer. Only the Holy Spirit can make these timeless truths come alive and have the power to convert and transform a person. It would be so helpful to study these truths and memorize all the verses presented in *italics*.

1. The Need of Salvation: Man's Sin.

All we like sheep have gone astray; we have turned, every one, to his own way...

Isaiah 53:6a

For all have sinned, and come short of the glory of God.

Romans 3:23

In these two verses the Bible clearly gives us the human condition. All have sinned. All have gone astray. No one is exempt. Before we can lead a person to Christ, we must convince them that they are sinners and that they need a Saviour. They will need to realize that they are drowning before they will want to be rescued and that they are lost before they will want to be found. The Lord Jesus told us what to "preach" when He expressly instructed, *"Repentance and remission of sins should be preached in His name to all the nations, beginning at Jerusalem,"* (Luke 24:47).

Since it is the **Holy Spirit's** task to *"convict the world of sin, and of righteousness, and of judgment"*, (John 16:8), **we need to pray earnestly** that **He** will give us what to say (and that **He** would perform **His** great task). We must not convey a "holier-than-thou" attitude! We may feel led to tell of how we were convinced that we had fallen far short of God's standards. A good illustration is to ask whether it is acceptable for a cook to serve an omelet made of nine good eggs and one rotten egg. In the same way, it would be an insult to God to present ourselves before

Him if we had **any** rotten deeds or thoughts in our lives. We could also use God's law as a *"tutor to bring us to Christ, that we might be justified by faith,"* (Galatians 3:24). Start with the first commandment *"...to love the Lord with all your heart, with all your soul, and with all your mind,"* (Matthew 22:37). Ask the person whether they have managed to keep that commandment and if not, explain that they need then to be forgiven – they need a Saviour.

2. The Ground of Salvation: Christ's Work

For God so loved the world that He gave His only begotten Son, that whoever believes in Him should not perish but have everlasting life.
John 3:16

All we like sheep have gone astray; we have turned, every one, to his own way; And the Lord has laid on Him the iniquity of us all.
Isaiah 53:6

Christ died for our sins according to the Scriptures.
1 Corinthians 15:3

After a person has been convinced that they are a sinner, then we must present the ground of God's salvation. It is a most wonderful illustration to take any book and place it on your one hand. Then explain that the Bible says that our sin has formed a barrier between us and God – and point with the other hand to the book and then to above the book (to God). Now hold the other hand level with the hand that has the book. Explain that this empty hand represents Jesus Christ who has no barrier of sin between Him and His Father (God). Looking at the hand with the book, quote the verse, *"All we like sheep have gone astray; we have turned, every one, to his own way"*, then as you transfer the book to the other hand, *finish the verse "And the Lord has laid on Him (on Jesus Christ when He hung on the cross of Calvary) the iniquity (wrong doing) of us all,"* (Isaiah 53:6).

You can do this two or three times – until you feel convinced that the Holy Spirit has revealed to the person the enormous transaction that took place on Calvary's cross. Explain that just before Christ died, He cried out, *"It is finished,"* which can also be translated, "It is completely complete" or "It is fully paid – the debt of every individual person on earth has been settled – once and for all." Jesus Christ, by dying and then rising from the dead has become our One and only Saviour. The ground of mankind's salvation is Christ's finished work.

3. The Way of Salvation: Faith in Christ

For God so loved the world that He gave His only begotten Son, that whoever believes (trusts, has faith) in Him should not perish but have everlasting life.

John 3:16

For by grace (unmerited favour) you have been saved through faith, and that not of your own doing, it is the gift of God, not of works, lest anyone should boast.

Ephesians 2:8,9

Therefore, having been justified by faith, we have peace with God through our Lord Jesus Christ.

Romans 5:1

The following is a powerful illustration – of a young lady who ran up huge debts. Because there was no way that she could pay, her creditors were taking her to court. Meanwhile, she falls in love with a young man who asks her to marry him. She explains that that would not be possible, as she was sure to go to prison for her debt. He comes with her to the court where, after the swearing in, the judge asks her how she pleads. She pleads guilty. The judge then tells her that he has great news for her – someone, at great personal sacrifice, has paid her debt in full. Would she accept that? She is overwhelmed but then fears that there would be strings attached. So she says, "It depends on who paid the debt for me." The judge first gets the approval of the young man and then tells her who it was – the young man she wanted to marry! The strings attached would be a lifetime together! Of course she accepted! The judge then declares her innocent of all charges and she walks completely free into the arms of her "saviour".

In the same way, we all stand guilty before God who is our judge. We have a debt we owe Him that we could never repay. We plead guilty and He says, "My own Son, Jesus Christ, has paid your debt in full – do you accept that?" The "strings attached" are a lifetime with Him – for better, for worse; for richer, for poorer; in sickness and in health. If we say "yes" then God will pronounce us "innocent" of all charges. This is what "justification by faith" really means. Justified equals "just-as-if-I'd never sinned". We have a brand new start with no more guilt and shame – and no more fear of punishment. Then show them John 3:16, "*For God (the greatest person) so loved (the greatest love) the world (the greatest number of people) that He gave His only begotten Son (His greatest gift), that* **whoever (the greatest invitation) believes (trusts, has faith) in Him (the greatest power on earth)** *should not perish (the greatest disaster) but have everlasting life (the greatest future)."*

Just as we put our faith in the cars we travel in, in the food we eat etc. so God wants us to put our faith in His Son – and we do this by receiving Him into our lives as our personal Saviour and asking Him to forgive all our sin and then to occupy the throne of our lives so that we will now live for and by and with Him.

"But as many as received Him (Jesus Christ), to them He gave the right to become children of God, even to those who believe (trust, have faith) in His Name."

John 1:12

Invite the person to read this verse with you and then ask them whether they would like to pray this prayer,

"Lord Jesus, I acknowledge that I am a sinner – I have gone astray, I have gone my own way. I do believe that God laid on You all my wrongdoing, and that on the cross You paid in full the penalty of my sin. You rose from the dead and now invite me to receive You as my personal Saviour. I am so sorry for my past; I turn away from my sin, and I invite you into my life as my personal Saviour. Please cleanse me of my past sin and please sit on the throne of my life as my Lord, to order my future. I now want to follow you and live for you."

Now show them John 1:12 again and say to them, "You have just received Jesus Christ, haven't you?"

"Yes!"

"Now – what does the Bible say here that you are?"

"It says that I am a child of God!"

"Is that not truly wonderful? Let me show you a couple more verses."

You turn to Acts 3:19 and ask them to read it with you, *"Repent (turn right around) and be converted (return to God), that your sins may be blotted out (erased, wiped clean), so that times of refreshing may come from the presence of the Lord"*. Now say, "You have turned right around and returned to God, so what has happened to all the sins of your past?"

"They are blotted out!"

"Wow! You are now a child of God, and your past sins have been blotted out! That calls for a prayer of thanksgiving and praise!"

Now you lead them in glorious praise to God for this great transaction you have just witnessed.

4. Assurance of Salvation: God's Word

These things have I written to you who believe in the Name of the Son of God, that you may know that you have eternal life.

1 John 5:13

For God so loved the world that He gave His only begotten Son, that whoever believes (trusts, has faith) in Him should not perish but have everlasting life.

John 3:16

My sheep hear my voice, and I know them, and they follow Me. And I give them eternal life, and they shall never perish; neither shall anyone snatch them out of my hand.

John 10 :27,28

We must make it perfectly clear that assurance is not obtained because of any feelings that may be ours; assurance is always based on the Word of God. It is when we believe God's Word that His Holy Spirit bears witness with our spirit that we are the children of God (Romans 8:16). In 1 John 5:13, God does not say, "These feelings I have given you"; He says, *"These things I have written."* He does not say, "That you may hope or think or feel that you have eternal life"; He says, *"That you may know that you have eternal life."* He does not say, "That you are going to have eternal life"; He says, *"That you have eternal life."* In other words, the assurance of salvation is based on what is written. Salvation is a knowable experience and a present possession. It is vital that the new convert leaves with the assurance of their salvation – only then will they be in a position to share their faith with others.

5. Immediate Follow-Up

We need to encourage the new convert to:

a. Pray and Praise

Ask, and it will be given to you; seek, and you will find; knock, and it will be opened to you.

Matthew 7:7

God is now their Father, and He wants them to talk to Him about anything, anytime and anywhere. Explain the acrostic for faith – Father-All-In-Thy-Hands and encourage them to entrust all their plans, problems, difficulties, concerns, loved-ones, friends, neighbours, etc., to Him. Give personal testimony to answered prayer. Encourage them to praise God for who He is and for what He has done and is doing. Since sin will be the only thing that will break communication with God, show them 1 John 1:9 which says, *"If we confess our sins, He is faithful and just to forgive us our sins and to cleanse us from all unrighteousness."* Tell them that it will take time for them to become like Jesus Christ. In the meantime they will be tempted, and will sin. Therefore this verse will apply daily to them. It contains a most spectacular promise.

b. Read and apply God's Word

As newborn babes, desire the pure milk of the Word, that you may grow thereby.

1 Peter 2:2

Encourage them to begin reading the New Testament in the order God has set – from Matthew. If they ask God before each reading to open their eyes and hearts to His Truth, and show them how to live for

Him, they will grow as Christians to bring God much joy. They should read until He speaks to them – it may be the first verse they read or it may be after a number of chapters. Bible-reading is to be two-way communication. "Talk to God about what He is saying to you." If you have *Every Day with Jesus for New Christians* or *Word for Today* or *Daily Bread* or *Now You Are a Christian* or *How to Live the Christian Life* or testimony books such as *The Cross and the Switchblade*, *The Hiding Place*, and *Run Baby Run*, then lend or give them a copy. Arrange to meet with them in the next week to further encourage them, answer any questions they may have, and pray/praise together.

c. Gather together with fellow Christians

We know that we have passed from death to life, because we love the brethren (fellow Christians).

1 John 3:14

The convert will find they have a completely changed attitude toward Christians and church. That is one of the most significant signs of their conversion. You may encourage them to become involved in a local church/Christian group where Jesus Christ is worshiped and the Bible honoured. Explain what Christian fellowship and encouragement have meant to you. In the very likely event that they want to come to your fellowship, arrange to meet them at the door, sit with them through the meeting, and introduce them to your pastor and Christian friends.

d. Share your faith with others

If you confess with the mouth the Lord Jesus and believe in your heart that God has raised Him from the dead, you will be saved. For with the heart one believes to righteousness and with the mouth confession is made to (confirm) salvation.

Romans 10:9,10

The convert will know that there is no turning back once they have confessed to anyone that they have accepted Jesus Christ as their Saviour, Lord, and friend. Confession seals/confirms the great transaction. Often the convert will want to tell another Christian first. That's good! No doubt the Christian they tell will be overjoyed and very encouraging. It is generally preferable and more fruit-bearing to encourage the convert to share his new faith with non-Christians only when they ask questions.

But set apart the Lord God in your hearts, and always be ready to give a defence to everyone who asks you a reason for the hope that is in you, with meekness (humility) and fear (respect).

1 Peter 3:15

The first duty is to show practical love and to pray for their non-Christian family, friends, and neighbours. Questions and methods of sharing their new-found faith can be tackled in follow-up at which time baptism in water (a great public confession of faith) and in the Holy Spirit (to receive power to be the Lord Jesus' witness) can also be discussed.

Conclusion

Every person on earth is unique. Every one is loved and valued by God, and He knows exactly how to win them into a personal relationship with

Himself. It is therefore of paramount importance to ask for His wisdom every time we share His truth. Pray too for "Divine appointments" and opportunities. Be aware that a spiritual battle occurs every time we share God's love and truth. So pray before, during, and after every opportunity. Walk humbly with your God and so allow Him to use your life and your lips. Then you will experience the unspeakable joy of being used by Him to bring in the rewards for His sacrifice on Calvary's cross.

God bless you, and may His love and passion for the lost inspire and motivate you!

Appendix B
A Study on How to Forgive

The Lord Jesus, in giving a model for daily prayer, said,

> *And forgive us our debts, As we forgive our debtors... For if you forgive men their trespasses, your heavenly Father will also forgive you.*

And here is the scary bit,

> *But if you do not forgive men their trespasses, neither will your Father forgive your trespasses.*
>
> Matthew 6:12-15

We are also told,

> *And be kind to one another, tenderhearted, forgiving one another, even as God in Christ forgave you.*
>
> Ephesians 4:32

This appendix is designed to briefly explain how to forgive! To do this we divide the offences into two categories – small (easy to forgive) and great (hard to forgive). Simple but profound illustrations are used in this highly practical study. You may, however, require in-depth counselling for some of the great (hard to forgive) offences. The release, the freedom, the healing, and the joy of forgiveness is too wonderful and life-changing for words!

1. Small (easy to forgive) Offences.

*And whenever you stand praying, if you have anything against anyone, forgive him **and let it drop – leave it, let it go** – in order that your Father who is in heaven may also forgive you your failings and shortcomings and let them drop. But if you do not forgive, neither will your Father in heaven forgive your failings and shortcomings.*

Mark 11:25,26 (Amplified Bible)

These verses give a wonderful illustration of how to forgive small offences – such as not putting the cap back on the tooth-paste tube; failure to show appreciation for hard work; expressions of irritation; excuses and lies; laziness and so on. Picture writing these offences down on a piece of paper and then holding that piece of paper to the offender's back. That is where we most often hold the "charge sheet" – where the offender cannot see it, but where we can!

They may be aware that we have something against them, but they do not know what! We no longer look them in the eye, the relationship is adversely affected, and the offender may not know why. That is plainly unfair! If we are to tell them the offence(s) (and Matthew 18:15 tells us to *"…tell him his fault between you and him **alone**…"*) our motive should always be to do so in such a way as to help them and win them back (*if he hears you, you have **gained** your brother*).

Often when the offence is small or petty we endeavour to build up a case through the destructive and dangerous practice of fault-finding. We also often make it harder for us to reconcile by letting others know of these offences. Often when the offender detects that we have something against them, they find things to hold against our back – and we end up going around and around in circles with neither being able to look the other in the eye. A once precious relationship can be severely damaged unless one takes the initiative to forgive and reconcile.

It is very often when we find ourselves having the same or similar faults to the one who has offended us that we do what the verse above tells us to do – we let the "charge sheet" drop to the floor, and we leave it there. We do not want to be judged by the same measure we have judged them (Matthew 7:1,2) and we want to be in relationship with them again – and so we let it drop, leave it, let it go.

Perhaps the greatest motivation we have to forgive others their failures and shortcomings towards us is the knowledge that Almighty God has forgiven us all our failures and shortcomings towards Him. He laid all our iniquity on His beloved Son when He sacrificed His life on Calvary's cross. God's justice was satisfied there, and He is eager to forgive and justify all who place their trust in Christ and His finished work on the cross!

Another motivation is God's repeated command to us all to forgive and His warning that His willingness to forgive us is conditional upon our willingness to forgive others! Our commitment to love another flawed human being will have to also carry our commitment to time and time again forgive them. That is a fact of life this side of heaven!

2. Great (hard to forgive) Offences

There are offences such as betrayal, infidelity, slander, incest, violence, childhood abuse, rape, abandonment, and so on, which are not easy to let drop, leave, or let go. These are a huge debt which, if simply dropped, would leave us with the keen sense of bankruptcy and injustice. Our right sense of justice makes us want the offender to pay dearly for his crime. We are afraid that letting go would effectively "let them off scot-free." There is a wonderful solution which brings us true freedom, and the offender true justice.

Once again picture writing the offences down on a "charge sheet" and then holding it against the back of the offender. This time you cannot simply let it drop and leave it on the floor. Instead you call upon your Heavenly Advocate, Jesus Christ, to hold the "charge sheet" against the offender. 1 John 2:1,2 says, *"My little children, these things I write to you, so that you may not sin. And if anyone sins, we have an Advocate with the Father, Jesus Christ the righteous. And He Himself is the propitiation for our sins, and not for ours only but also for the whole world".*

The acrostic for faith is **F**ather **A**ll **I**n **T**hy **H**ands or alternatively **F**or **A**ll **I T**rust **H**im. To place the "charge sheet" into His Hands will require faith. Should we trust Him to handle this matter? The Biblical answer is "yes!" Romans 12:19-21 (Amplified Bible) says, *"Beloved, never avenge yourselves, but leave the way open for [God's] wrath; for it is written, 'Vengeance is Mine, I will repay (requite),' says the Lord. But, If your enemy is hungry, feed him; If he is thirsty, give him drink; For by so doing you will heap burning coals upon his head. Do not let yourself be overcome by evil, but overcome (master) evil with good."*

Vengeance is not an evil thing, or it would not be given in Scripture as God's prerogative. By handing the "charge sheet" to our "Advocate with the Father" we are in fact leaving the way open for God's wrath (fierce anger). We often find that when we do that our attitude towards the offender changes to one of profound sympathy, and we may say with the prophet *"In (Your) wrath remember mercy,"* (Habakkuk 3:2). Steven, in Acts 7:60, feels such sympathy for those stoning him that he *"...cried out with a loud voice, 'Lord, do not charge them with this sin.' And when he had said this, he fell asleep (in death)."*

It is highly probable that the early church were in the habit of placing all in His hands – including offences such as persecution and all its attendant evils. Hence the Lord Jesus, when confronting Saul of Tarsus on the road to Damascus, did not say, "Saul, Saul, why are you persecuting my church?" but rather, *"'Saul, Saul, why are you persecuting Me?' And he said, 'Who are You, Lord?' Then the Lord said, 'I am Jesus, whom you are persecuting. It is hard for you to kick against the goads,'"* (Acts 9:4,5).

The Biblical fact is that Jesus Christ is personally offended whenever we are, (Luke 10:16) *"He who hears you hears Me, he who rejects you rejects Me, and he who rejects Me rejects Him who sent Me."* And He warns us in Matthew 18:6,7 *"Whoever causes one of these little ones who believe in Me to sin, it would be better for him if a millstone were hung around his neck, and he were drowned in the depth of the sea. Woe to the world because of offences! For offences must come, but woe to that man by whom the offence comes!"*

Once we are trusting our Advocate to hold the "charge sheet" to the back of the offender, we can step back in sheer relief that the matter is now between the Lord Jesus and the offender and no longer between us and the offender! The Lord Jesus will definitely hold the offender to account for the wrong done to us (*"Vengeance is Mine, I will repay (requite)," says the Lord*) (Romans 12:21) unless the offender sincerely repents before God and apologizes to us. (Acts 3:19,20 says, *"Repent therefore and be converted, that your sins may be blotted out, so that times of refreshing may come from the presence of the Lord."*)

God does not forgive the offender just because we have forgiven them. He only forgives them when they repent and change (are converted)! Praying for that repentance to come to the offender is the best way to *"overcome (master) evil with good."*

Forgiveness is not easy in many a case. We will be tempted to take matters back into our own hands. That temptation is from the devil and needs to be resisted. In many cases the offences are multiple, and we need to commit every offence (as and when they come to mind) to the Lord Jesus for Him to handle them on our behalf – as the Advocate with the Father. Such childlike faith He rewards with His joy, peace, freedom and dignity! It also frees Him to set about healing our wounded emotions and our wounded soul. That can take time. In every case we need to echo Abraham's words in Genesis 18:25, *"Shall not the Judge of all the earth do right?"*

How do we know that we have really forgiven?

We know that God has forgiven us not because we cannot remember our sins (they form part of our history and testimony) but because God's forgiveness has freed us from guilt, shame and the fear of His punishment. His peace rules in our hearts. Romans 5:1,2 (Amplified Bible), *"Therefore, since we are justified – acquitted, declared righteous, and given a right standing with God – through faith, let us [grasp the fact that we] have [the peace of reconciliation] to hold and to enjoy, peace with God through our Lord Jesus Christ."*

We know that we have forgiven someone their sin against us not because we cannot remember their sins (they form part of our history and testimony), but because we no longer feel anger, resentment, bitterness, malice, vengeful, or restless. We have a peace, confidence and contentment that our Advocate, Jesus Christ, is handling the matter perfectly on our behalf. We may even be praying for them, blessing them, and doing them good!

What about Reconciliation?

It takes one person to forgive but two persons to reconcile! That is what the Lord Jesus was talking about in Luke 17:3,4, *"Take heed to yourselves. If your brother sins against you, rebuke him; and if he repents, forgive him. And if he sins against you seven times in a day, and seven times in a day returns to you, saying, 'I repent,' you shall forgive him."* Also read Matthew 18:15-18, *"Moreover if your brother sins against you, go and tell him his fault between you and him alone. If he hears you, you have gained your brother. But if he will not hear, take with you one or two more, that 'by the mouth of two or three witnesses every word may be established.' And if he refuses to hear them, tell it to the church. But if he refuses even to hear the church, let him be to you like a heathen and a tax collector. Assuredly, I say to you, whatever you bind on earth will be bound in heaven, and whatever you loose on earth will be loosed in heaven."*

Reconciliation that is not superficial or artificial, but deep and real, requires the offender to fully acknowledge not only the offence(s) but also how deeply the offence(s) have hurt us. This requires a face to face and heart to heart discussion. Caution: we need to be sure we are ready and willing for such a confrontation. We need to state clearly to the offender that the reason for the discussion is that we want a good relationship with them – we want reconciliation. The timing is crucial as such a confrontation will often backfire if the offender is arrogant, hostile or irritable.

We need to have built up our inner strength, and we need to be well rehearsed in what we will say. Having said our piece in a gentle, calm, but firm manner we need to give the offender what is called "reaction time." This time can range from a few minutes to a few days. We must not back down or pretend it's now OK when we know it is not. Neither should we allow ourselves to be drawn into other often unrelated issues. Better to stick to our issue and promise another time to discussing the other issues.

All the time we need to pray that the Holy Spirit will soften the offender's heart and give us His wisdom! If they do not "hear" us then we should take along a witness. If that does not bring reconciliation (and the person is in the church), we are to then bring the matter to the church (leadership). If there is still no reconciliation then we will have to go our separate ways and relate on a different level.

The word repent in Luke 17:3,4 means to turn around and away from the wrong path – to leave that path behind – to take up God's path and live life God's way. Sorrow and grief are involved and sincere apologies are in order! In other words, reconciliation is not proof of forgiveness! Forgiveness is commanded – we have no option; reconciliation is conditional – sadly, this side of heaven, it does not always happen!

The Lord Jesus prayed for those who nailed Him to the cross, *"Father forgive them, for they do not know what they do,"* (Luke 23:34). Sadly this did not mean that He was reconciled to them although that is the message of the cross – 2 Corinthians 5:18-21, *"Now all things are of God, who has reconciled us to Himself through Jesus Christ, and has given us the ministry of reconciliation, that is, that God was in Christ reconciling the world to Himself, not imputing their trespasses to them, and has committed to us the word of reconciliation. Now then, we are ambassadors for Christ, as though God were pleading through us: we implore you on Christ's behalf, be reconciled to God. For He made Him who knew no sin to be sin for us, that we might become the righteousness of God in Him."*

Conclusion

Therefore, as the elect of God, holy and beloved, put on tender mercies, kindness, humility, meekness, longsuffering; bearing with one another, and forgiving one another, if anyone has a complaint against another; even as Christ forgave you, so you also must do. But above all these things put on love, which is the bond of perfection. And let the peace of God rule in your hearts, to which also you were called in one body; and be thankful. Let the word of Christ dwell in you richly in all wisdom, teaching and admonishing one another in psalms and hymns and spiritual songs, singing with grace in your hearts to the Lord. And whatever you do in word or deed, do all in the name of the Lord Jesus, giving thanks to God the Father through Him.

Colossians 3:12-17

We could conclude with so many wonderful stories of the freedom, the joy, the inner calm, the transformation that comes to those who forgive. We pray that after reading and applying the advice here you too would have a remarkable story of your own! May our forgiving God enable each of us to become as forgiving! God bless you!